Nuances of Technique in Dynamic Psychotherapy

Selected Clinical Papers

by
Mardi J. Horowitz, M.D.

Jason Aronson Inc.
Northvale, New Jersey
London

Library of Congress Cataloging-in-Publication Data

Horowitz, Mardi Jon, 1934–
    Nuances of technique in dynamic psychotherapy / Mardi J. Horowitz.
        p.   cm.
    Bibliography: p.
    Includes index.
    ISBN 0-87668-859-8
    1. Psychotherapy.   2. Psychotherapist and patient.   I. Title.
RC480.H63   1989
616.89′14–dc19   89-30865
                                                                                CIP

Manufactured in the United States of America. Jason Aronson Inc. offers books and cassettes. For information and catalog write to Jason Aronson Inc., 230 Livingston Street, Northvale, New Jersey 07647.

For my mother,
Lillian Horowitz—
A lovely woman of many nuances

The author gratefully acknowledges permission to reprint the following:

Chapter 1, "Levels of Interpretation." Original title: "Levels of Interpretation in Dynamic Psychotherapy," published in *Psychoanalytic Psychology*, vol. 3, pp. 39–45, copyright © 1986 by Lawrence Erlbaum Associates, Inc. Reprinted by permission.

Chapter 2, "Microanalysis of Working Through." Original title: "Microanalysis of Working Through in Psychotherapy," published in *The American Journal of Psychiatry*, vol. 131, pp. 1208–1212, copyright © 1974 by The American Psychiatric Association. Reprinted by permission.

Chapter 3, "The Therapeutic Alliance with Difficult Patients." Co-authored by Charles Marmar, M.D. and Mardi J. Horowitz, M.D. Published in the *Annual Review*, vol. 4, R. E. Hales and A. J. Frances, eds., Washington, DC, copyright © 1985 by the American Psychiatric Press, Inc. Reprinted by permission.

Chapter 4, "Visual Thought Images in Psychotherapy." Published in the *American Journal of Psychotherapy*, vol. 22, pp. 55–59, copyright © 1968 by the *American Journal of Psychotherapy*. Reprinted by permission.

Chapter 5, "Visual Imagery and Defensive Processes." Published in the *International Journal of Psychoanalytic Psychotherapy*, vol. 6, pp. 99–112, copyright © 1977 by Jason Aronson Inc. Reprinted by permission.

Chapter 6, "Phase-Oriented Treatment of Stress Response Syndromes." Published in the *American Journal of Psychotherapy*, vol. 27, pp. 506–515, copyright © 1973 by the *American Journal of Psychotherapy*. Reprinted by permission.

Chapter 7, "Character Style in Stress Response Syndromes." Original title: "Stress Response Syndromes: Character Style and Brief Dynamic Psychotherapy," published in the *Archives of General Psychiatry*, vol. 31, pp. 768–781, copyright © 1974 by the American Medical Association. Reprinted by permission.

Chapter 8, "Sliding Meanings in Narcissistic Personalities." Original title: "Sliding Meanings: A Defense Against Thread in Narcissistic Personalities," published in the *International Journal of Psychoanalytic Psychotherapy*, vol. 4, pp. 167–180, copyright © 1975 by Jason Aronson Inc. Reprinted by permission.

Chapter 9, "Cognitive Structure and Change in Histrionic Personality." Original title: "Hysterical Personality: Cognitive Structure and the Process of Change," published in the *International Review of Psycho-Analysis*, vol. 4, pp. 23–49, copyright © 1977 by the Institute of Psycho-Analysis. Reprinted by permission.

Contents

**Part Two
Nuances of Interpretation**

Acknowledgments

These clinical papers were selected and brought together for the first time because they describe a domain of concern for the individual style and capacities of the patient. The source of information was not only my own experiences in treating patients, but the opportunity to supervise other therapists and to review with colleagues the videotapes, audiotapes, and process notes from treatments in research contexts. For this very special opportunity I gratefully acknowledge long support through grants from the National Institute of Mental Health, the American Psychoanalytic Association, and the John D. and Catherine T. MacArthur Foundation.

I have modified these contributions in some ways, often by deletion of unnecessary material, but have found myself still able to stand by my previous assertions. Amy Wilner helped me in this editorial process. Nancy Wilner edited several of the manuscripts before they were published. My son Jordan Horowitz helped me with several of the bibliographies, as did Nancy Wilner. My longstanding colleague Charles Marmar discussed many of the salient issues with me over several years and co-authored the chapter on the therapeutic alliance, which also was influenced by Robert Rosenbaum during his postdoctoral fellowship with me.

Finally, I am grateful to the editors and mangers who published the original works and gave permission that this book might be made available.

Introduction

The basic techniques of psychodynamic psycho-therapy are well known. How they are used depends on the individual characteristics of the patient. This variation according to individuality or typology is what I mean by "nuances."

Several points of view on nuances of psychodynamic technique are presented. The first point of view concerns *level of interpretive work* by the therapist.

Chapter 1 examines eight levels of interpretation from which a clinician selects one to use at any given time. In so doing, he or she conceptualizes the optimum level of depth for a particular patient dealing with a specific theme. The surface level is defined in terms of the *current situational structure*, that is, the consciously known internal and external sources of current stress and conflict. Levels descend from there in terms of dealing more and more with the clinician's inferences about what the patient does not consciously comprehend. At the deepest level, interpretations are framed about the dynamic unconscious.

Dealing with successively deeper layers during a psychodynamic psychotherapy may help a patient to gradually integrate previously incompatible or dissociated memories, fantasies, values, self concepts, and motives. Conflict resolution means an interfacing of wishes, fears of the implications of wish gratification, and defensive warding off of wishes to avoid such threats.

The second chapter deals with emotional themes and focuses on how one may integrate more conscious thoughts with usually warded-off unconscious potentials for thought and action. Chapter 2 introduces a *format for microanalysis*, one that the reader might use on his or her own clinical material to analyze the associations between current ideas and enduring attitudes and dynamic constellations of ideas, emotions, and defenses.

The depth of interpretation that may be helpful to a patient in terms of ability to integrate conflicts that generate negative emotions depends in large measure on the nature of the current relationship with the therapist as perceived by the patient. The better the *therapeutic alliance*, the more the patient can tolerate the conscious experience of negative emotions. The patient has a lessened dread of entering an out-of-control or undermodulated state of mind.

The importance of the relationship is a central theme in psychoanalytic psychotherapy. Transference reactions are a focus of the therapist's attention, if not always the theme of an interpretation. Part of the problem of technique in dynamic psychotherapy concerns the impedances caused by transferences in establishing a therapeutic alliance with difficult patients. An approach to analyzing the *dilemmas* of transference with such difficult patients is presented in Chapter 3.

Provided that a therapeutic alliance can be established and that the context is one in which explorations toward a deeper level of interpretation would be helpful, the therapist may begin to add nuances of technique that deal with how the patient experiences usually warded-off or excessively intrusive emotional themes. Chapters 4 and 5 focus on how to use shifts in modes of representation from verbal expression to visual imagery and how then to describe subjective imagery in clear verbalizations, obtaining a cross-translation that reduces defensiveness and increases insight. Chapter 5 deals especially with nuances of technique that may help a patient set aside defensive inhibitory operations. The chapter compares interpretive and directive interventions as options for use by the therapist.

Because visual images are close to perception and memories of perception, and because they may be less subject to conscious self-regulatory efforts, there is a tendency for persons under stress to experience intrusive and repetitive imagery about emotional themes. Exploring that tendency led me to clinical research on stress response syndromes and a reconsideration of unconscious defensive processes that in therapy function as resistances to working through conflictual themes. Therapeutic techniques for clarifying and dealing with such resistances are presented in Chapters 6 through 8. These chapters deal especially with ways to formulate the psychodynamics of such cases and the nuances of interpretation and of establishing a therapeutic alliance with patients who have histrionic, compulsive, and narcissistic styles. Microanalysis is again used to provide a conceptual model of conflict in emotional themes. Ideas and emotions are not regarded as products of separate modular mental systems but as united into constellations of meaning and schemas.

Chapter 9 explores one of these typological styles, the histrionic, and reviews all the nuances of technique covered in earlier chapters in terms of how they may integrate to facilitate a change in mental schemas, emotional themes, and defensive style. As in the earlier chapters, the effort is a new synthesis of an object relations psychoanalytic point of view with both classical psychodynamics and theory from cognitive psychology. This volume contains previously published papers on this topic. I am grateful to the publisher, Jason Aronson, for surveying two decades of my work and inviting this specific collection.

Mardi Horowitz
San Francisco, 1988

PART ONE

THE THERAPEUTIC
PROCESS

1

Levels of
Interpretation

Research on brief dynamic psychotherapy has raised interesting questions about levels of interpretation. These issues pertain, but in a less pressing manner, to the conduct of long-term therapies of this sort. In brief therapies, such as a time-limited dynamic therapy for stress response syndromes, a focus is usually in order. Even when that focus concerns reactions to a recent serious life event, such as a death or rape, there is

5

inevitable meshing of the patient's individuality and the situational episodes. How far to clarify the patterns of unconscious reactions and how much to stay on the surface structure of events are patient-specific questions and puzzling ones to many therapists.

Clinical work and the literature on brief therapy range in their depth of prototypical interpretation. There is general agreement that this issue of depth of interpretation ranges somehow from a surface clarification of the patterning of events to an attempt to understand patterns that are schematized and functionally active at the level of unconscious mental structures and processes. Some brief therapies aim to clarify for the patient his or her core, unconscious, nuclear conflicts. Some brief therapies aim at working through a recent stress event. All tailor what the patient can handle to the individual situation and moment. Discussion of this range has been hampered by the lack of a system to further define what is meant by such surface to depth levels of interpretation.

LEVELS OF
INTERPRETATION

In a somewhat arbitrary way, although stemming from the detailed study of individual therapies and quantitative efforts to develop therapist action scales, eight levels will be discussed. The individual therapy analyses are available elsewhere (Horowitz et al. 1984, Horowitz 1987) as are the quantitative studies (Hoyt et al. 1981, Horowitz et al. 1984). The eight levels are crudely arranged from the surface of situational analysis to the depth of warded-off unconscious impulses and agenda. They are as follows:

1. Situational thematic structures, as illustrated in the combination of external stress events and the stress responses of the individual, are the most superficial level of interpretation. Such interpretations include ordering for the patient the sequences and causal relations of life events and emotional responses.

2. Pending coping choices and conscious scenarios are the next level of interpretation and are illustrated in the extension of the therapeutic interpretations from examination of stressors and stress responses to the individual's consciously contemplated plans of response. This includes a clear statement of the patient's dilemmas about which of several alternative, conflicted choices to make as personal action responses to the stressful situation.

3. The avoidance patterns in which the individual does not confront adaptive challenges are the topic of somewhat deeper levels of interpretation. These avoidances are not necessarily unconscious, but they are seldom fully center stage in the sphere of conscious attention. Thus movement to this level involves interpretation of themes that are warded off by the patient consciously and unconsciously. Obviously, this level of interpretation can still be focal, if it deals with a specific life stress situation and pending coping choices.

4. Repertoires of states of mind may also be interpreted in terms of how current problems and symptoms are em-

bedded in a given state of mind and how that state of mind relates to the habitual states of mind of the individual. By examining these habitual states of mind, one can relate a current stressful situation to personality, albeit at a relatively superficial level of analysis. This allows development of an interpretation of defensive operations as well as motivations. That is, the states of mind desired and dreaded by the person can be related to those that are currently frequent and problematic, and those that are defensively stabilized in order to avoid entry into dreaded states. Usually the person will not have thought consciously about his or her own personality in terms of such configurations, although depth interpretation of unconscious motives is not involved at this level.

5. A closely related level of interpretation deals with conscious thoughts that are usually concealed from social communication and perhaps, early episodes of communication even with a trusted therapist. This level concerns expressed irrational beliefs, ones which may stand side by side with the patient's more rational attitudes. The irrational belief may not be unconscious but, as with the avoidance of adaptive challenges, it may not be clearly represented. The interpretations of the therapist provide the clear representations of beliefs that permit their comparison with other, perhaps more rational views.

6. The next level moves from a stress event related focus to one of personality patterns as manifested in repetitive maladaptive interpersonal behavioral patterns. This is the bread and butter of change in long-term therapies and often is an essential feature of brief therapies. Yet it cannot be assumed that this level of interpretation is invariably

valuable. The patient must be able to use the information gained in adaptive ways. Many of the techniques of dynamic therapy extend this level of interpretation from analysis of current outside situations to examination of the same patterns in the past history of important formative relationships, and to relationship patterns observed— moreover as felt by the therapist—in the therapy situation itself.

7. Analysis of repetitive interpersonal behavioral patterns leads generally to a somewhat deeper analysis, to examination of the recurrent self-concepts and views of others that are enduring schemata in the mind of the patient. These repertoires of self-concepts, object concepts, and role relationship models are not fully conscious. Rather, they act as unconscious organizers of sequences of experience and behavior. Yet views of self and others can be represented consciously, and that conscious recognition can help the person modify impulsive and defensive configurations.

8. The deepest level concerns warded-off, unconscious scenarios and impulsive agendas. I mean this language to include drives, preemptory biological needs, and powerful scripts. These deeper levels are the patterns that lead to the powerful but unexpected surges of emotion during mourning, the mystery of dreams, the sudden solution of long-stymied problems through creative explosions, and to self-mortification at times of apparent success or approaching triumph. This is, then, interpretation of what might be called the demonic or angelic unconscious, for we still do not understand all its patterns although we attempt, at times, to interpret what we can.

ARENAS OF PATTERN RECOGNITION

The eight levels of interpretation, as so briefly and fragmentarily described, and as separated by arbitrary lines, are represented as a vertical dimension in Table 1-1. A horizontal dimension is also provided. It includes the three arenas of pattern observation mentioned with the discussion of repetitive maladaptive interpersonal behavioral patterns. These are current external situations, the current therapy situation, and past situations. As it happens, these three arenas are appropriate to consider at any level of interpretation.

If the reader will grant the arbitrary nature of the divisions selected, this establishment of rows and columns allows for boxes into which a few illustrative themes in therapy can be placed. At the deepest level of interpretation, the examination of current extratherapy situations involves an approach to patterns found in sudden urges, unbidden images, dreams, and creative products. In terms of the patterns noted in therapy, the most prominent theme in the literature is interpretation of a regressive transference neurosis, as in psychoanalysis. In terms of past patterns, the conflicted, dynamic unconscious scenarios and agendas are examined in terms of unfolding, developmental patterns and choices, as punctuated in illuminating ways by episodes of regression in which usually warded-off aims are more clearly revealed.

Going back to the most superficial level, we can examine the current situation in terms of interpreting how the patient intends to cope with stressors. The stressful situation can also be examined in terms of patterns of

TABLE 1-1. Levels of Interpretation

Content areas	Level of Analytical Focus		
	Current situation	Therapy situation	Past
1. Stressors and stress responses	Intentions of how to respond	Expectations of treatment	Relevant experience of previous stress events
2. Pending coping choices and conscious scenarios	Conflicting aims of how to respond	Dilemma analysis of what to deal with first	Long-standing goals and habitual conundrums
3. Avoidance of adaptive challenges	Threat and defense	Resistance to working through a conflicted issue	History of self-impairing character traits
4. Repertoire of states of mind	Triggers to entry into problem states or exit from symptomatic states	States of therapeutic work and nonwork	Habitually problematic and desired states
Link between external situation and personal responses			
5. Expressed irrational beliefs	Differentiation of realistic from fantastic associations and appraisals	Differentiation of realistic from fantastic attributions	Differentiation of memory from fantasy elaborations
6. Repetitive maladaptive interpersonal behavior patterns	Interpersonal problems and self-judgments	Difference between social alliances, transferences, and therapeutic alliances	Abreaction or reconstruction of traumas and strains in relationship
7. Self-concept repertoires and role relationship models	Views of self and others	Differences between social alliances, transferences, and therapeutic alliances	Development of role relationship models
8. Warded-off unconscious scenarios and impulsive agendas	Urges, dreams, and creative products	"Transference neurosis"	Episodes of regression that uncovered warded-off aims in the past
Link between current problems and long-standing individualized personality patterns			

reacting to the therapy situation itself. This domain includes interpretations of what the patient expects of the
treatment. History can be examined for patterns of how
similar stressors were experienced and how reactions to
them occurred in the self, or in figures of developmental
importance.

CONCLUSION

The therapist may search for important maladaptive
patterns in the therapy situation, as well as in the current
situation, and in the history of the past. The redundancy in
the pattern allows the therapist to recognize the important
features. The rate of interpreting the given pattern to the
patient will depend on how that patient can process and
react to the interpretation. The domain of *observation* by
the therapist is not necessarily the domain in which the
therapist first *interprets* the relevant issues to the patient.
This applies both to starting with a more superficial level of
interpretation and working as deeply as possible, and to
starting with the current external situation and working
into recognition of patterns in the therapy and the past. By
examination of levels and zones of interpretation, as shown
in Table 1-1, the therapist may consider what is optimum
for a given patient at a specific phase of the treatment
process. This consideration is one of the important nuances
of how the technique of psychotherapy may be varied to
suit the developmental level or particular state of the
patient.

REFERENCES

Horowitz, M. J. (1987). *States of Mind: Analysis of Change in Individual Personality*. 2nd ed. New York: Plenum.

Horowitz, M. J., Marmar, C., Krupnick, J., Wilner, N., Kaltreider, N., and Wallerstein, R. (1984). *Personality Styles and Brief Psychotherapy*. New York: Basic Books.

Horowitz, M. J., Marmar, C., Weiss, D., DeWitt, K., and Rosenbaum, R. (1984). Brief psychotherapy of bereavement reactions: the relationship of process to outcome. *Archives of General Psychiatry* 41:438–448.

Hoyt, M. J., Marmar, C., Horowitz, M., and Alvarez, W. (1981). The therapist action scale and the patient action scale: instruments for the assessment of activities during dynamic psychotherapy. *Psychotherapy: Theory, Research, and Practice* 18:109–116.

2

Microanalysis
of
Working Through

With an eventual goal of an improved rationale for therapy, it is desirable to clarify the cognitive processes involved in the theoretical construct of "working through." A detailed microanalysis of episodes in therapy is one step toward this goal.

I analyze a single episode – the composition of a poem during a session of psychoanalytically oriented psychotherapy. As it happened, many classical psychodynamic principles were illustrated in this episode, but the microanalytic approach provides the details of only one. For example, the poem formation helped the patient to master a conflict, and the degree of anxiety experienced was titrated by a series of defensive operations, particularly a temporary denial that allowed a gradual integration of warded-off ideas. The microanalysis focuses on this gradual integration.

The compulsive repetition of stress-related ideas, the emotional valence attached to recent experience because of childhood experiences, and the reproduction of these experiences in the dimensions of transference and resistance are also relevant themes but are not the focus for the present microanalysis.

The detailed focus on the gradual expression in consciousness of threatening ideas will mean a discussion of the regulation of which ideas gain mental representation, the organization and shifts of organization of thought, changes from a concrete personal instance to an abstract concept, and fluctuations in self and object awareness.

BACKGROUND

In the early period of psychoanalysis, working through was discussed in terms of pathogenic traumatic experiences and instinctual demands. After interpretation and preliminary insights, working through entailed further recollection and repetition. This resulted in abreaction of emotional responses previously "strangulated" by repression. Included in the concept was progressive confrontation, as well as modification of the power of unconscious instinctual demands (Freud 1914).

With the rise of ego psychology, working through came to mean a repetitive overcoming of unconscious defensive patterns as they appeared in current experiences and were recognized in the patient's memories of the past (Greenacre 1956). In contemporary psychoanalysis, a cognitive point of view adds further details to the concept of working through. Included in the elaboration of associative meanings of current and past memories and fantasies is the revision of attitudes, as well as the modification of self and object representations. I will focus on only a sector of working through concerned with the extension of meanings of a current life event, especially the relationship between the current ideas and past ideas, emotional responses, and reactive defenses.

CASE FRAGMENT

The patient, a student in his late 20s, lived as an intellectual hermit. Although he was brilliant, he was socially immature and professionally unsuccessful. "Narcissistic personality disorder" would be the closest diagnosis. The episode of interest occurred during the second year of psychoanalytic psychotherapy.

A comment on the patient's style of working in therapy at this stage of treatment will clarify the context of the vignette. He characteristically brought in an emotionally toned current experience. He would not know clearly what the emotions were or why the experience bothered him; we were to find that out together. We would then "find out" that the experience gave rise to ideas that wounded his self-esteem and caused sadness, fear, humiliation, anger, or self-disgust. He would then parade the negative emotion in an exhibitionistic way, enjoying this activity as a sign of his successful work in treatment and as evidence of my attention and "gifts of insight" (a narcissistic transference gratification) (Kohut 1971, Oremland and Windholz 1971). As will be seen, this form of interpersonal relationship paralleled the content of the warded-off ideas and feelings.

In previous hours he had worked sporadically – to a degree that was tolerable for him – on his fear of the various rituals of sexual courtship. When he was forward in caresses, he felt in danger of a humiliating rejection; when he was backward, he felt in danger of being labeled as nonvirile. An arrogant nonchalance was a common pose to maintain poise and self-esteem.

He began the hour by talking about the previous evening spent with a girlfriend. He was characteristically nonchalant as he mentioned, almost as an aside, that he had engaged in intercourse with her for the first time. The incident he brought in for this hour was that he had noticed that "something haunted him about the occasion." This incident occurred a moment prior to intercourse. They had undressed themselves some feet apart from each other and he had seen her glancing at him. He recalled thinking of himself, "I have a handsome and tanned head but my body must look old because it is white and soft."

After telling me of the haunting quality of the memory, of the glance, and his idea of a young head on an old body, he then entered a reverie state, which was his narcissistic version of free association. I call his reverie state "narcissistic" because I had reason to believe that he experienced it as if he were a child asleep and dreaming while I, the parent, watched and guarded him. This was in fact an idealizing quasi-transference (Kohut 1971). During the experience he had no sense of me as a cohesive person other than as a kind of two-dimensional "guardian." Also, in this state, he seemed to have little or no sense of reflective self-awareness (Schafer 1968).

In this reverie state, which will be called the "experiential mode" in what follows, he reexperienced the event through a revisualization of the scene. He described again the idea of his body being old and his head young. He made the association of "old" as "unattractive"; he supposed the girl might find his white body old and unattractive.

Warded-off Contents

Now, I deviate from chronology to describe the warded-off mental contents in order that the reader may know the ideas and feelings that the patient was predisposed to have at this point. These emergent contents were warded off because they threatened to cause excessive emotional pain if they were directly and clearly experienced. The contents emerged only gradually through the progressive integration of defense and threatening contents (Sampson et al. 1972, Weiss 1967). I hope the reader will bear with a dense statement of the entire warded-off cluster, since this will clarify the functions of the construction of the poem.

The *conscious idea*[1] "My body is white" and the implied

---

[1]The italicized phrases refer to areas printed in capital letters in Figure 2-1. This figure is best used as a flow chart read piecemeal while the reader is following the text.

"She may find it unattractive" tended to evoke the *respondent idea* "My body will really age" (as outlined at the top of Figure 2-1). This idea was warded off first through repression and then through denial (as diagrammed by the broken lines in Figure 2-1 and described later in terms of specific cognitive maneuvers).

Why was the idea "My body will really age" warded off? Because it matched associatively with an *enduring attitude.* "Only the young get attention" — an attitude based in turn on oedipal *memories* (how he succeeded in diverting his mother's attention from his father, who was old) and fantasies (according to the talion principle, his punishment for replacing his father will be to age as he has). There is also a plausible preoedipal configuration, although I do not have sufficient evidence to be sure of this: his mother did stop treating him as "his majesty the baby" as he grew from infancy to childhood, and she later indulged (as the patient experienced it) a younger sibling.

The associational match led to the "conclusion" that he would not get attention. This *respondent idea* "He will not get attention" is a narcissistic blow in that it does not mesh well with an appraised (although warded-off) need for continuous attention from others. The threat of experiencing such thoughts in conscious form generates signal anxiety related to a fear of the loss of the object's love or the loss of the object. The composite *emotional experience* would be potentially intolerable if inhibitory *controls* (for the moment crudely summarized as denial and repression) did not prevent a clear conscious representation of the *respondent ideas.* In the model diagrammed in Figure 2-1, emotions are responses to ideational matches and in turn motivate control of ideation.

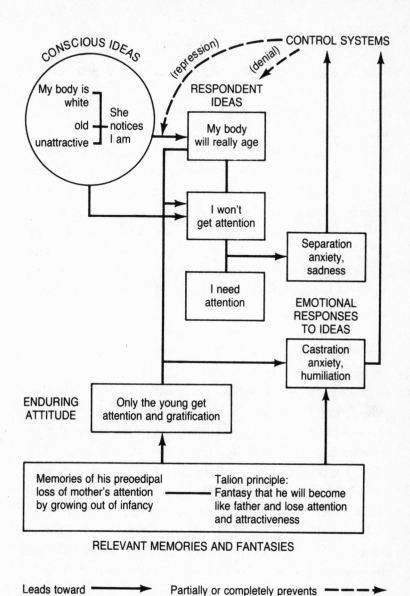

FIGURE 2-1 A Prototype of the Ideational Structure

Cognitive Maneuvers

Now let us return to the stream of experience described by the patient in the hour with me. He was in a state of thinking the *conscious ideas* and warding off the *respondent ideas* shown in Figure 2-1. His repressive capacity—the ability to totally inhibit the "My body will really age" idea—was not adequate to the emergent power of this associative idea. He experienced this idea consciously but then denied its import in a series of cognitive maneuvers. The composite of these maneuvers, which were spoken of summarily above as "denial," accomplished two aims. They titrated his conscious emotional experience to within tolerable limits, and they also led eventually to a clear and conscious expression of the once warded-off ideas.

The first noticeable maneuver was to change the concrete personal image of the girl looking at him, and even the less object-oriented idea of his body aging, to an abstract principle—not "My body will age" or "My body is older," but "Bodies age." Concomitantly, he shifted modes or plans of thought organization from an experiential mode (experiencing his associational responses) to a problem-solving mode (thinking of the implications and possible recombination of the associations with reference to a particular goal) (McGuire 1971). In particular, he switched to a problem-solving mode of formulating a poem. Poetic organization of a certain type was familiar to him—he liked to compose three-line haiku. The organizing format or "goal" of these poems was to juxtapose two seemingly contrasting ideas to arrive at a third line that synthesized the two contrasting ideas.

In this problem-solving mode he therefore had a predetermined and automatized plan: Take the idea "Bodies age," find a potentially related but opposite idea to juxtapose, and then show the relatedness of the two ideas. This switch from responding in an experiential mode to operating in a problem-solving mode temporarily halted the ideational cycle of linear associations that would lead to representation of the warded-off contents (Horowitz 1970, Klein 1971). Instead, he now "knew" what else to think: If "Bodies age" represents a loss, he had to think of a relevant gain. He selected sensibility, a kind of wisdom of the body, as the gain with aging. The loss (attractiveness) and gain (sensibility-wisdom) juxtaposed well with a poignant, bittersweet, evocative quality in the short poem. (The three ideas were "Bodies age," "One gains sensibility-wisdom with time," and "The second compensates for the first.") The poem "read" well and he felt a thrill imagining an audience's response. There was, again, a narcissistic gain to compensate for a narcissistic loss.

While I am constrained not to report the actual poem, a similar substitute has been contrived. Although it is not as aesthetically pleasing as the original, it conveys the ideational movement.

Old hawk wings droop with time yet hover still
Sharply sudden the deft swoop through needles' eyes
How expertly this ancient warrior pierces his target prey

As he imagined the audience or reader response, he switched from the problem-solving mode—filling ideas into the plan for a haiku—to the experiential mode. This experiential mode consisted of the contemplation in fantasy of how someone else would respond emotionally to his poem.

In the context of this return to the experiential mode, he then experienced anxiety and sadness in an attenuated form—as poignancy that was tolerable because something was gained as well as something lost. This emotional experience was not clearly located; it was neither in his self nor in his imagined audience but somehow partook of both. There was, however, a relative reversal of roles from passive to active. Next, he again switched modes away from the experiential organization of thought sequence. He went from the experiential mode, his reverie of associational responses, to the analytic mode. That is, he became aware of me and himself again (reflective self-awareness). He then reflected on my responses to the poem, which will be described after a brief summary of matters thus far.

To recapitulate, this patient titrated a gradual emergence and experience of warded-off mental contents by a series of cognitive maneuvers. These maneuvers involved: (1) inhibition of representation of the warded-off contents; (2) change from a personal, concrete instance to an abstract concept; (3) change from an experiential mode (allowing responsive associations) to a problem-solving mode (composing a poem); (4) decrease in reflective self-awareness and awareness of my presence; and (as awareness of me returned) (5) associations of *my* possible responses to the haiku and to ideas of *my* aging.

Assimilation

As he thought of my response, he decided that I was old and therefore "whiter" and "softer" than he, but that maybe I could take it because I had accumulated wisdom. This externalization allowed him continued partial immunity from the emotional threat, but it also allowed him to contemplate the warded-off ideas and feelings and to appraise the degree of threat through identification with me. Could I stand it?, etc. From this point of view, the construction of aesthetic symbols or "names" serves contemplation of emotion rather than intense and direct experiencing of emotional states (Langer 1942).

Deciding that I was all right (that is, not too threatened by either the thrust of his powerful creative achievement or my comparative age), he switched modes from the analytic mode (thinking of what went on between us) to the experiential mode (associative reverie). He developed associations clustered around his *enduring attitude* that only the young can get attention, and getting older pushes you "off stage." There was then a brief disavowal of the topic — he was not old but young — and another return to the hard-to-accept idea that he too would really age. There were then switches between modes. These went from his associative reveries to the analytic mode ("What would I think of his associations" — his version at this point of an observing autointerpretive ego) and back to further associations that led eventually to his conscious experience of the warded-off contents.

Toward the end of the hour, then, he had the capacity to think and feel contents that had been warded off earlier in the hour. His shift to writing poetry allowed a period of what could summarily be called denial, although there was actually a composite of defensive maneuvers. During this period he progressively assimilated threatening ideas and feelings. The poetry writing, in particular, entailed a switch away from the experiential mode, an alteration in self-object attitudes, and a wishful, narcissistic compensation for a threatened blow to his self-esteem.

At the end of the hour he stood up and announced he would write down the poem and that he had "really gotten something" from this hour. This savoring of "getting" and his capacity to make the poem reassured him: He had a safe retreat. In a way, he could tolerate the threat of the warded-off contents only in the real relationship and the narcissistic transference (me as guardian angel and receptor of bad things, like age). Wrapped in a package, the poem, the warded-off ideas, and our relationship could be reviewed and yet denied, a way station on the path to integration and acceptance.

What was worked through? Some previously warded-off ideas and feelings about a particular life event and related past experiences were allowed representation. This permitted the event to be assimilated or worked through. His style of avoiding threatening ideas and feelings by denial and repression was not altered by the one hour, but repetition of such work gradually increased his tolerance for painful ideas, cut down generalizations based on childhood experience, and reduced the extensiveness and intensiveness of his unconscious defensive operations. His defensive style, narcissistic vulnerability, and enduring attitudes were chipped away at, not worked through. As for the transference situation, this hour was a repetition. Once again he paraded a "discovered" negative emotion in an exhibitionistic way. The transference perhaps evolved a little and, together with realistic goals of self-awareness, motivated the working through of the stressful life event. But the patient gained no insight into the transference aspects of this hour, and they were not interpreted at this time in the treatment.

THE CASE FRAGMENT IN
THE LARGER CONTEXT
OF THE THERAPEUTIC
PROCESS

This chapter has focused on cognitive maneuvers in a single hour. If it were a fully developed case report, the focus would have been on longer-order patterns, such as the patient's use of an idealizing transference to bolster an impairment in maintaining a cohesive self-concept. The psychoanalytically oriented reader may tend to enlarge on the small-order patterns in order to imagine the large-order patterns involved in the patient's character pathology and may wonder what interpretations were involved in the treatment. As it happened, no interpretations were made by the therapist in this particular hour. The therapist operated as a presence—only partially experienced by the patient, but nonetheless a presence—who occasionally (like a rudder) made quite minor deflections that kept the patient safely on a course. These few comments on the treatment are made only to clarify what is not under discussion here: transference, resistance to transference, interpretation of transference, genesis, and resistance.

Interpretive activity did precede and follow the hour. Alone, the patient would not have extended the meanings of the stressful event because the emotional threat (anxiety and/or humiliation) was too great. In the therapeutic rela-

tionship, the emotional threat was reduced, and the anticipation of transference gratification motivated an elaboration of ideas and feelings that were usually warded off.
Interpretations of resistance and fears about intimacy,
trust, and self-exposure had preceded this moment in therapy. Such work led to the existing alliance, the protective
umbrella of relationship that allowed the patient to work
out his ideas without immediate interpretation.

During the hour reported I felt it advisable not to
interpret those meanings of the material that were too
threatening. The patient's sense of self-esteem and safety
was enhanced by his own capacity to work out the event
and its significance, once confidence was present. In subsequent hours it was possible to return to the memorable
product, the poem, and elaborate further meanings.

For example, the episode of intercourse was a major
stress as well as an accomplishment. The patient's anxieties
about sex and performance were as important as, or more
important than, his worries about his appearance. He was
afraid of being judged inferior, and the hawk and prey diad
of the poem was symbolic of a particular self and object
schema. One role was that of a strong, sadistic aggressor,
the other of a helpless, faceless, or amorphous object.

The poem was a wish fulfillment. It posited him as the
hawk, the woman as "prey." He was capable of "piercing"
fully and was not in danger of impotence. The self-object
diad was a reversal of the most fearful version of the same
schema, in which he was the characterless prey. The clarification of this aspect of the episode, as well as certain
sadistic aspects of his sexuality, required subsequent interpretation and much more extended working through.

CONCLUSION

Microanalysis focuses on the small-order patterns of the interrelationship among ideational structure, emotional responses, and reactive control responses. Several tools for microanalysis can be abstracted from the method used in this single case. The feedback system between ideas, emotions, and defenses involved a particular format in which the discrepancy between current ideas and enduring attitudes generated affect. The threat of painful emotions motivated control systems, which inhibited or distorted the ideational structure, leading to a decrease in responsive affect. A reduced threat of affect, resulting from controls, alterations in the mode of thought organization, or safety in the relationship, allows the amplified consciousness of usually warded-off ideas.

This format suggests a diagrammatic structure that can be used for other types of microanalysis. Minute clarifications, if multiplied, can lead to a theory of the processes of change in psychotherapy. In turn, such knowledge would lead to improvements in techniques.

Technique often involves focusing conscious attention of the patient through interpretations or suggestions that alter the controls of the patient. When such unconsciously instituted controls are used by a patient in such a way as to gradually reduce defensive avoidance, the therapist may remain as a useful, silent presence, as in the present example from a single hour. At other times, subtle nuances of technique may be used to alter controls in the direction of a working-through process.

REFERENCES

Freud, S. (1914). Remembering, repeating, and working through. *Standard Edition* 12:145–156.

Greenacre, P. (1956). Re-evaluation of the process of working through. *International Journal of Psycho-Analysis* 37: 439–444.

Horowitz, M. J. (1970). *Image Formation and Cognition*. New York: Appleton-Century-Crofts.

Klein, G. S. (1967). Peremptory ideation: structure and force in motivated ideas. *Psychological Issues* 5:80–128.

Kohut, H. (1971). *The Analysis of the Self: A Systematic Approach to the Psychoanalytic Treatment of Narcissistic Personality Disorders*. New York: International Universities Press.

Langer, S. (1942). *Philosophy in a New Key*. Cambridge, Mass.: Harvard University Press.

McGuire, M. T. (1971). Dyadic communication, verbal behavior, thinking and understanding. III: Clinical considerations. *Journal of Nervous Mental Disorders* 152:260–277.

Oremland, J. D., and Windholz, E. (1971). Some specific transference and supervisory problems in the analysis of a narcissistic personality. *International Journal of Psycho-Analysis* 52:267–275.

Sampson, H., Weiss, J., and Mlodnosky, J. (1972). Defense analysis and the emergence of warded off mental contents: an empirical study. *Archives of General Psychiatry* 26:524–532.

Schafer, R. (1968). *Aspects of Internalization*. New York: International Universities Press.

Weiss, J. (1967). The integration of defenses. *International Journal of Psycho-Analysis* 48:520–524.

3

The Therapeutic Alliance with Difficult Patients

with Charles Marmar, M.D.

There is at the present time little empirical information that would allow one to describe the characteristics of a difficult patient. Instead, it is helpful to regard difficulty as a feeling that emerges either in the therapist or in some other clinician who reviews the psychotherapeutic process. The experience of dealing with a difficult patient may be recognized as a sense of foreboding when approaching or anticipating an interview with a certain patient or as a sense of frustration during a session, and often manifests itself in a communication to colleagues such as "I just had a session with a difficult patient." While colleagues know what is meant, the details of that difficulty and how to handle it are considerably less clear.

For certain therapists, a specific type of patient may be the most difficult. Some therapists feel especially stymied or frustrated when dealing with patients who are highly suspicious, very angry, demanding, or dependent, or who have conflicts that are active and unresolved in the therapist himself. For most therapists, it is not the sickest patients who are necessarily the most difficult. Rather, difficulty seems to result from a composite of traits affecting the relationship that can be established between the patient and therapist. With a difficult patient, establishing a therapeutic alliance is a formidable and perhaps an impossible task.

The difficult patient is one who not only presents transference phenomena but a problem in recognizing the realistic aspects of the actual treatment situation. Myerson (1977, 1979) has reviewed the clinical descriptive literature and has provided an important summary formulation. He follows Balint (1968) and others in describing the therapist's subjective experience of difficulty. It is as if, when one is dealing with a difficult patient, there is a shell surrounding that patient. Because of this insulation the therapist feels screened off, left out, unable to connect. The metaphor uses a "hard," interposed, protective shield because the "shell" is not simply due to unfamiliarity with the opportunities for honest expressiveness provided by the usual psychotherapeutic situation. It is not modified by the patient's chance to learn that the therapist is a safe person with whom to discuss ideas and feelings. Similarly, the shell is not due to a justifiable early alertness to seeing whether this therapist is a good one or not. Instead, the shell is carried about, from one relationship to the next, from this therapist to that one, and constitutes not only a part of the patient's difficulty, but an obstacle in the path of work upon that difficulty.

The role-relationship model that is manifested by the shell is formed, as Myerson describes it, in early development. The important figures, such as parents, in that development may have been either overstimulating and intrusive, or more likely they have been ungratifying, as well as unwilling or unable to mitigate the distress of the child who grows up into the patient. The shell is a character defense based on the expectation that the other person cannot or will not help, and/or that the other person will be invasive in a dangerous manner.

The particular type of shell discussed by Myerson and others is especially frustrating because it does not fulfill the hopes of the patient. The patient, when alone, can imagine a close relationship in which there is a helpful, mutual, give-and-take of honestly disclosed ideas and feelings. When with someone, as when with the therapist, this imagined closeness cannot be established. There is a frustrating difference between the relationship expected when the patient is alone, and the relationship that the patient can actually offer when not alone. This frustrating difference between the two models of relationship is transmitted to the therapist in the process of either blaming the therapist, or signaling to the therapist that the patient does wish to establish a closer contact, but cannot do so.

The presence of these difficulties has been felt to be especially high in persons with narcissistic or borderline personality organizations, as described by Hartocollis (1977), Horowitz et al. (1984), Kernberg (1975), Kohut (1977), Modell (1976), and Winnicott (1965).

Patients at this level of personality organization tend to have high state mobility (as, for example, with rapid and unstable shifts from rage to hopelessness, to paralyzing guilt or terrifying emptiness), uncontrolled surges of emotion, distortions in the perception of intentions of other persons, a tendency to regressive shifts in self and object representations, and to present in polysymptomatic syndromes that shift over time. Most authors, however, in recognizing this composite of attributes, do focus on the difficulty as the therapist's sense of frustration in establishing the kind of relationship that the therapist would like to establish, and usually does establish. This relationship has been described as the therapeutic alliance. In order to discuss further the difficulty in establishing a therapeutic alliance, it is helpful to contrast this model of a relationship with two others: the social alliance and transference relationships.

ROLE RELATIONSHIP MODELS IN PSYCHODYNAMIC PSYCHOTHERAPY

Any individual patient can be described in terms of varied role-relationship models that he or she may use to organize expectations and intentions as they take place during psychotherapy. Generalizing across patients, we see that three types of relationship models may characterize the transactive patterns as conceptualized by either party. The therapeutic alliance is a term used to designate that relationship pattern in which both the patient and therapist have the shared goal of understanding and resolving the patient's problems. The therapist is characterized as an expert, the patient as a person motivated to seek and to obtain help from that expert. The aim of each party is a mutual give-and-take that will lead to gradual, full disclosure of problems, and discussion of possible modes of their solution in relationship to "if/then/but" blocks to their solution.

Transference relationship phenomena have been well described and lie at the very core of the psychodynamic approach to psychotherapy (Freud 1912, 1914, Gill 1982). The transference relationship models may be composed of varied negative and positive intentions or expectations. They are derived from wishes and fears based on earlier experiences and unconsciously transposed into the psychotherapy opportunity. This is not necessarily antitherapeutic; instead, comparison of the role-relationship models of a *therapeutic alliance* with the role-relationship models of the manifested transference relationship allows for insight and modification.

A third type of relationship model in psychotherapy is the *social alliance* (Horowitz 1987). The social alliance may serve as a resistance to establishing a therapeutic alliance, for it is based on a role-relationship model that might take place were the two parties to meet in ordinary life, but not for the purposes of psychotherapy. The social alliance might have aims between the parties of friendly conversation about matters of mutual but superficial interest, banter, sexuality, or a coalition to criticize some third party.

These three models of relationship—the therapeutic alliance, social alliance, and transference relationship—all involve some kind of "transference" in terms of their formation. That is, any role-relationship model used to organize expectations, appraisals, and intentions in an interpersonal transaction will derive elements from the repertoire of schematic forms carried into the situation by the patient and the therapist. The therapeutic alliance is formed on the basis of a choice of elements within an available repertoire, the elements that most closely resemble the realistic possibilities within the ground rules of what constitutes dynamic psychotherapy. The social alliance deflects from these aims of therapy as therapy, substituting instead the aims and scripts of courtship, friendship or games.

In patients who are not perceived by therapists as being especially difficult, dynamic psychotherapy proceeds by interpretations of the social alliance when it serves as a resistance to the therapeutic alliance, and of transference as an inappropriate set of ideas and emotions based on past but not necessarily current realities or fantasies. The therapy proceeds with a gradual deepening of the therapeutic alliance; in that deepening it loses some of the properties transferred from preexisting role-relationship models imposed upon the situation, and schematizes the new transactional properties found in the growing mutuality and intimacy of the actual therapeutic give-and-take. Deepening and developing the role-relationship model of the therapeutic alliance is, in and of itself, one of the advances made in the course of the psychotherapy, for it involves development of the patient's self-concept and his or her capacities for relating with others. In difficult patients there is some type of impasse interfering with this type of development and deepening.

One of the major early findings in clinical observation of dynamic interchanges was that transference manifestations did not necessarily obstruct the aims of symptom resolution and improved adaptation in relation to personal problems. Instead, the manifestation of transference-relationship models, the allowance of regression, and expression of usually warded-off wishes and fears often created an opportunity for deepened insight and working through of conflicts to points of new decision. Interpretation of transference became one of the key ingredients in psychoanalytically oriented psychotherapy.

Nonetheless, the facilitating effect of transference interpretation was not found in all cases. In a difficult case, as noted by Myerson (1977), the usual efforts at transference interpretation often have little positive effect and may possibly have a negative effect. Horowitz and colleagues (1984) have reported some empirical evidence supporting the clinical impressions reported by Myerson (1977) and have summarized impressions by other clinicians and psychotherapy researchers. Especially in cases where at treatment onset there is low motivation and reality relationship capacity in the patient, transference interpretations may not lead to a deepening of the therapeutic alliance.

In summary, then, it may be stated that the utilization by the patient of either a social alliance or transference-relationship model for organizing the expected or intended relationship between patient and therapist is not necessarily a source of difficulty. Either of these impositions can be interpreted and contrasted with the potentials for a therapeutic alliance, leading to gains. Impasses occur when social alliances or regressive transferences are imposed and there is interference with this route to change. In such instances the therapist recognizes the presence of an impasse.

IMPASSES

In an empirical analysis of elements in the psychotherapeutic process, Orlinsky and Howard (1975) distinguished five kinds of impasse. These included: unproductive contact, which is similar to Myerson's (1977) concept of the "shell" as a prevention to relatedness; defensiveness; ambivalent nurturance-dependence aims leading to excessive and frustrating dependency; uncomfortable types of involvement; and conflictual erotization. Themes such as ambivalence, dependency, and erotization do not necessarily complicate therapy. But they do lead to impasses when they are caught up in the kind of conflicts suggested by Orlinsky and Howard. That is, there might be some kind of double-binding situation tying up both the patient and the therapist.

The double bind, in this formulation, is present not only in the patient, but as Kiesler (1979) has pointed out, is evoked in the therapist by means of "command messages" sent by the patient and reacted to unconsciously by the therapist. Strupp has indicated such factors, as well, in the difference between success and failure in dynamic psychotherapy (Strupp 1980). Lang has written extensively about this type of impasse (1975, for example). Ryle (1979) has offered an especially illuminating formulation, writing at just about the same time as Myerson.

Ryle defined what he called "dilemmas, snags, and traps" as various types of impasse in psychotherapy, and offered these as potentially key focal concerns that might center attention in brief psychotherapy. Stimulated in part by the work of Kelly (1955) on personal constructs, and based on his own empirical research using the repertory grid technique (1975), Ryle defined dilemmas as false dichotomizations into "either/or" expectations or excessively limited, or rigid "if/then" kinds of beliefs. Ryle gave examples of two common dilemmas. In one of these, the patient feels that "in relationships I am either close to someone and feel smothered, or I am cut off and feel lonely." The second example would be stated by a patient like this: "I feel that if I am feminine, then I feel that I have to be insensitive" (pp. 47–48).

Ryle is aware that such dilemmas have long been described in the psychoanalytic psychotherapy literature, and that sometimes they are even used to describe particular kinds of personality disorder (as in DSM–III). The progressive aspect of the work, as found in other cognitive approaches such as those reported by Beck (1967, 1976) is that the actual propositions in these patterns are clearly stated in a way that is not only pertinent to an individual, but may also represent a typology or set of patients.

As already mentioned, Ryle divided impasses into dilemmas, snags, and traps. He defined traps as the result of relating to others in terms of such "either/or" or "if/then" dilemmas. One of the examples that he gave features the alternatives between being accommodating or unreasonably angry. As a patient might word this, were it conscious and clear as a pattern: "I am unduly accommodating to others; the result is that I often feel abused or invaded by them and this leads to my being irritable or unreasonably angry; as a result of this anger, I feel guilty and that makes me unduly accommodating to others." The trap is that the person cannot escape from this cycle but is ensnared within it. Therefore, Ryle defines a snag as an obstacle to change that results from the combination of dilemmas and traps. It is like the third feature in a double bind that keeps the person from leaving the field. It says in effect, "I want to change, but if I do then the snag will be. . . ."

Following these definitions, Ryle identifies six main groups of dilemmas, snags, and traps. They can be summarized in this way:

1. A distance/closeness dilemma: Either the patient feels excessively isolated or at risk from being too close.
2. A controlled/controlling dilemma: The patient feels either helplessly submissive to another, or excessively powerful over another.
3. A must/won't dilemma: The patient feels that he either has to have feelings or to communicate ideas at the expense of being chaotic, or that he has to be in tight control, in which he cannot or will not reveal ideas and feelings that ought to be revealed according to the roles of therapy.
4. A forced choice dilemma: The patient feels that only two roles are being offered; that he or she must choose one or the other, with the loss of some opportunity in giving up one, when in reality there is an opportunity to select components of both roles and combine them in some way.

5. A trap in which a problematic role relationship can only be reversed, so either the self or the other is in a given role, such as being either aggressor or victim, with unacceptable consequences of being in either position.

6. A snag that usually involves a wish to enact some transaction with either a parent or sexual partner, coupled with a belief that such aims always lead to a bad consequence such as punishment, guilt, shame, or anxiety.

CONFIGURATIONAL ANALYSIS OF IMPASSES

A dilemma, in the sense provided by Ryle, would be exemplified by a patient who cannot remain in a social alliance, because then therapy would not proceed; but the patient cannot leave the social alliance, because then the more emotional give-and-take would lead into a feared transference-relationship model rather than a therapeutic alliance. A difficult patient would be one who could not imagine or project a therapeutic alliance, and would thus be trapped in this dilemma. Another aspect of a trap would be a situation in which the patient and therapist would endlessly blame each other, shifting roles as to who was guilty of failing to make the therapy "work."

A method for systematically formulating the different components of such forms of impasse has been called "configurational analysis" (Horowitz et al. 1984, Horowitz 1987). This method provides a series of steps and formats for description and explanatory clinical inferences about the states of mind, self-concepts, role-relationship models, and modes of processing information that take place within the therapy situation. It focuses on the integrative function of the mind, resulting from the interaction and conflict of multiple component functions.

Utilizing this method of explanatory description, we have identified compromise states of mind and role-relationship models that are used to prevent *both* establishment of the therapeutic alliance and the emergence of dreaded emotions in more regressive or projective relationship phenomena. We have located two types of difficulties that are pertinent to this discussion. One is a kind of impediment to the development of the therapeutic alliance generated by the active presence of regressive or projective role-relationship models. The other type of difficulty has to do with the absence of a superordinate self-concept and role conceptualizing system; in such a case, the patient cannot allow the kind of parallel processing that permits recognition of inappropriate but active relationship views to be simultaneously compared with reality, or with the actual possibility of a therapeutic alliance (Horowitz and Zilberg 1983).

In our detailed analyses of change processes in psychotherapy using the configurational analyses method, we have found that many such instances of impasse have three characteristics. These are

1. The patient indicates to the therapist that he or she should be more than usually active in order to facilitate a halting or disabled level of therapeutic work (as follows the finding of Kiesler 1979).

2. The patient then indicates to the therapist, often in a

barely conscious way, that there is some pitfall standing in the path of the very activity that is being solicited.

3. Unfortunately, in such patients that are found by the therapist to be difficult, there is hardly any zone of safety between either (1) ignoring the provocation or (2) responding to it.

The therapist is thus on the horns of a dilemma.

Dilemmas are best described with clinical detail such as analyzed transcripts from the individual psychotherapy. Such detail is provided elsewhere (Horowitz et al. 1984, Horowitz 1987), and so here a simple, general model will be provided. The first horn of such a dilemma can be illustrated by a patient who displays chaotic thoughts and intense fear and confusion, suggesting an inability to structure inner experiences, with difficulty in communication.

Such fear and confusion, signaled to the therapist, is not uncommon and does not lead to the sense of difficulty described here in the therapist. Instead it usually tends to call forth very positive responses in which the therapist helps the patient to focus on a line of thought and organize it into a coherent sequence of memories, responses, and plans. With an especially difficult patient, when the therapist answers the call for help in this usual way, something untoward happens. The therapist then encounters the second horn of the dilemma.

As described by Myerson and Ryle, the second horn occurs when the patient feels that the therapist is invading his or her autonomy and privacy, fears merger with the therapist, and so responds oppositionally. The therapist finds himself in a "damned-if-you-do and damned-if-

you-don't" position in response to these horns of a dilemma. When the therapist tries interpreting both horns
simultaneously, the patient becomes confused. Both parties
experience the session as difficult (and so does the supervisor or consultant).

A dozen sample dilemmas, following this form of two
horns, are listed in Table 3-1. These dilemmas have been
developed from configurational analyses and scrutiny of
videotapes by a team of colleagues seeking to specify such
dilemmas. It is not an exhaustive list, but it does illustrate
this approach. At the present time we seek to determine if
clinicians can reach consensual agreement as to whether a
given dilemma is present on a given segment of recorded
psychotherapy and, if so, to analyze the process of its
solution. The example just given is listed as the first of these
dilemmas.

An expanded view of the first dilemma listed in Table
3-1 is provided by the following example. A nonworking
state of mind indicates the need for some change in the
therapy situation. We will refer to this state as that of *social
chit-chat*. In this state, the patient's self-concept is presented
as that of a peer aiming at friendly interchange, to pass the
time amiably with the therapist. The therapist is viewed as
if a casual companion by the patient. During this social
chit-chat state of mind there is leakage of emotions—
anguish and rage over a recent loss. The slight, momentary
shimmers of these warded-off emotions activate the therapist to act against the resistence of the social chit-chat state.
This is the role-relationship model of horn *a* of the first
dilemma listed in Table 3-1.

A tentative series of efforts by the therapist does not
alter the social chit-chat situation and he then intervenes

TABLE 3-1. A Dozen Sample Dilemmas

1. **a.** The patient is constantly frightened of inability to structure inner experiences and control chaotic thoughts and emotions.

   b. *But if* the therapist attempts to structure the communication of these ideas and feelings, the patient will see this attempt as an invasion of autonomy and privacy, will fear domination or merger, and will oppose it.

2. **a.** The patient manifests helplessness and dependency upon the therapist for caretaking.

   b. *But if* the therapist addresses this attitude or indicates the necessity for assuming personal responsibility, the patient will feel so neglected or overwhelmed by demands that regression or withdrawal will follow.

3. **a.** The patient is so deflated and demoralized that very little impetus to engage in work is present.

   b. *But if* the therapist addresses this attitude or encourages the patient to a more positive view, then the patient will feel the therapist is too unempathic and unrealistically optimistic and will feel increasingly hopeless.

4. **a.** The patient feels entitled to more than the therapist can give within the usual boundaries of psychodynamic psychotherapy and so feels neglected and abandoned.

   b. *But if* the therapist allows boundaries to become flexible the patient will feel too special to have to work in therapy.

5. **a.** The patient exhibits a tendency or likelihood to act out.

   b. *But if* the therapist interprets this tendency as maladaptive and needing increased control, the patient will see that interpretation as criticism and become increasingly rebellious.

6. **a.** The patient does little besides repetitively express personal suffering.

   b. *But if* the therapist addresses this pattern and encourages other work, the patient will feel so misunderstood that only increased expressions of suffering or withdrawal will take place.

TABLE 3-1. A Dozen Sample Dilemmas *(Continued)*

7. **a.** The patient is so passive that all initiative is placed with the therapist.

   b. *But if* the therapist becomes active in fostering communication, the patient will comply dependently without processing meanings personally.

8. **a.** The patient maintains such a distance in regard to key issues that the therapist is not trusted with intimate communications.

   b. *But if* the therapist interprets the avoidance or encourages the patient toward increased intimacy, the patient will become fearful and back off further.

9. **a.** The patient is preoccupied with challenging the therapist to show competency and strength.

   b. *But if* the therapist addresses this challenge by reassuring the patient about an ability to tolerate whatever the patient expresses, the patient will either obstinately increase the level of the challenge or submit obsequiously and inauthentically.

10. **a.** The patient does not express some ideas and feelings central to core aspects of important topics.

    b. *But if* the therapist addresses this avoidance or mentions these warded-off ideas, the patient would experience the therapist's confrontation of a resistance as corrosively scornful criticism.

11. **a.** The patient presents in a contrived manner in which substitute emotions are used to hide more primary and authentic ones.

    b. *But if* the therapist confronts the defense and the warded-off affects, the patient will become confused.

12. **a.** The patient presents in an overcontrolled manner that avoids emotional expression.

    b. *But if* the therapist discusses this avoidance and the warded-off emotions, the patient will either be overwhelmed by experiencing them, or distraught with fear of being unable to tolerate the experience.

vigorously. Responses at such times indicate another role-relationship model, one underlying horn *b* of the dilemma. In this role-relationship model the patient is like a dangerously vulnerable, empty, and damaged person frightened by a ruthless invader and manipulator. This concept of the situation leads to a fearful, chaotic state of mind in which thoughts are experienced as confusing jumbles. The patient cannot process what the therapist means. As the therapist backs off, the patient gradually resumes the social chit-chat state of mind.

Between these two role-relationship models there was little zone of safety because there was no role-relationship model of cooperative mutuality in this patient's repertoire of mental schemata. Conflictual and infantile patterns of interpersonal behavior with both parents persisted into adulthood, and there were no restorative figures such as siblings or peers in her surrounding social network. (The absence of an intimate, equal relationship was compounded by never having had a good teacher-to-student relationship during school years.) There were few elements in the patient's repertoire upon which to build a therapeutic alliance. The therapist felt left out: his real attributes and the real opportunities in the situation were unrecognized, contributing frustration to his sense of difficulty.

Two impediments to development of a therapeutic alliance have been mentioned. One is generated by the type of linked and threatening expectations just explicated as the two horns of a dilemma. The second is the relative absence of supraordinate concepts of self and relationship. The patient in the present example has not fully developed a supraordinate self-concept, and an equivalent schematic form for synthesizing varied role-relationship models. As a consequence of this difficulty in psychic schematizations of meaning, it was hard for the patient to modulate one relationship view (one horn of the dilemma) with another (the relationship model characterizing the other horn of the dilemma). Thus the patient was entirely "in" one state or the other, with abrupt shift between states. This also meant that the therapist could not engage the patient in parallel processing, a simultaneous examination of both threatening relationship models involved in the dilemma.

EMPIRICAL STUDIES

Hartley (1985) and Luborsky and Auerbach (1985) have summarized psychotherapy research studies, indicating that aspects of the therapeutic alliance can be reliably measured. Our own work has followed such leads and found an empirical support for the clinical postulate that the alliance could be divided into patient and therapist relationship contributions, each with an enhancing (positive) or impairing (negative) component (Marmar et al. 1986). In a study involving fifty-two cases of pathological grief treated with brief dynamic psychotherapy, high levels of negating patient contributions were found to be associated with poorer outcome, controlling for the effects of pretherapy symptomatic severity (Horowitz et al. 1984). The dilemmas discussed may be an aspect of these alliance-impairing factors, as suggested by our intensive analysis of some cases in this sample using configurational analysis for descriptive explanation (Horowitz et al. 1984), and Strupp's (1980) intensive studies of paired cases, ones having good and poor outcomes, as treated by the same therapist.

The techniques that in clinical observations may help resolve dilemmas will be discussed below. Foreman and Marmar (1985) have studied in an empirical manner the techniques that might help reduce patient alliance-impairing relationship contributions. Their pilot study examined six cases from the sample of fifty-two mentioned above. Each of these six cases manifested high patient-negative contributions towards a therapeutic alliance early in the brief psychotherapy for neurotic-level mental disorders precipitated by a bereavement. Half of the cases assessed to have initially negative patient contributions to the therapeutic alliance went on to improve the alliance, and to have a favorable outcome. Half of the cases maintained patient-negative contributions to the alliance over the course of the brief therapy and had a poor outcome. The most salient and consistent finding that differentiated the two groups of three cases was that, in the patients who improved, the therapist had addressed the defenses of the patient against expressing feelings about relationships both in and outside of the therapy. It appeared that the alliance scores did not improve until the therapist did address the patient's defenses within the patient–therapist relationship pattern. Of eight therapist actions assessed, in each therapy session this was the only one that seemed to correspond closely to the time frame of the decline of scores for the patient's negative contributions to the relationship as assessed by independent judges. This empirical finding, in a pilot study of a small number of well-selected cases, accords with general clinical suggestions, such as those of Kernberg in discussing issues of technique for psychotherapy of the borderline patient (1975).

In order to study dilemmas of the relationship as

contributors to poor outcome in psychotherapy and to arrive at a method for early identification, we embarked on studies assessing the components and reliability of clinicians' assessments of patient difficulty; we used independent operations, assessments of such dilemmas as described in Table 3-1. The results of such quantitative studies indicated the validity, reliability, and predictive utility of the concept of dilemmas (Horowitz et al. 1988, Rosenbaum et al. 1986).

HOW TO HANDLE DILEMMAS

Understanding the components of an impasse in forming a therapeutic alliance is essential if the therapist is to resolve the situation. In many instances, a minor difficulty is handled intuitively by the therapist without conscious recognition of the obstacle in the path of deepening or developing a therapeutic alliance. Analytic review and understanding is indicated when the operation of intuition alone is not sufficient to resolve the difficulty.

A relationship dilemma can be analyzed in terms of the horns that lead to a "damned-if-you-do and damned-if-you-don't" response. Once both horns are identified, the therapist may then attempt to puzzle out a way to clarify for the patient a middle zone that does not enter fully into either of the threatening positions. As that middle zone of safety is developed, the therapeutic alliance is deepened; and the threat of either of the horns can be examined within that zone, the therapist utilizing the usual methods of helping the patient to reexamine events and to discriminate reality from fantasy projections.

This remedy is relatively straightforward with some difficult patients, but with the "difficult" difficult patients there is no middle ground; the horns of the dilemma overlap. When the therapist attempts to clarify the threat embodied within each horn of the dilemma, hoping to indicate the possibility for a therapeutic alliance between them, the patient instead feels impaled by both problems simultaneously. To avoid flooding the patient and risking a drop-out, the therapist may avoid excessive interpretation while at the same time avoiding being provoked into any action that could be interpreted by the patient as threatening relationship expectations. This leads to the type of empathic holding treatment described by Kohut (1977) and Modell (1976), and the principles of therapeutic change with persons of lower organizational levels of self-concept development, as described by Gedo and Goldberg (1975).

The goal of building a therapeutic alliance may be explicitly stated and discussed as a shared focus for attention during sessions. A hierarchy of technical approaches may build on this understanding. The first general tactic is to interpret horn *a*, the manifest surface of the dilemma, and to observe how the patient processes this information. The therapist may then add clear description of the potential alliance by repeatedly defining his own attributes, expectations, and intentions.

An important aspect of such an approach is to ask the patient what he or she has heard the therapist say. This inquiry aims to find out the patient's appraisals after the session as well as during it.

The next technique in this hierarchy of therapist

actions to counteract a dilemma is to interpret the *b* horn, the more hidden aspect of the dilemma. In so doing the therapist may, with the most difficult patients, say explicitly and repeatedly what safeguards are incorporated into the real situation to reduce this threatening expectation. The usual techniques of showing the activity, meaning, and developmental origin of the patient's negative expectations and transferences are used in this approach. The added emphasis is on helping the patient learn the real potentials and attributes of the relationship of the therapeutic alliance.

REFERENCES

Balint, M. (1968). *The Basic Faults: Therapeutic Aspects of Regression*. London: Tavistock.

Beck, A. (1967). *Depression*. New York: Harper & Row.

Foreman, S. A., and Marmar, C. R. (1985). Therapist actions that address initially poor therapeutic alliances in psychotherapy. *American Journal of Psychiatry* 142:922–926.

Freud, S. (1912). The dynamics of transference. *Standard Edition* 12:99–108.

———— (1914). Remembering, repeating, and working through. *Standard Edition* 12:147–156.

Gill, M. (1982). *Analysis of Transference: Theory and Technique*. New York: International Universities Press.

Hartley, D. E. (1985). Research on the Therapeutic Alliance. In *Psychiatry Update*, vol. 4, ed. A. J. Frances, R. E. Hales, pp. 532–549. Washington, DC: American Psychiatric Press.

Hartocollis, P. (1977). *Personality Disorders*. New York: International Universities Press.

Horowitz, M. J. (1987). *States of Mind*. 2nd ed. New York: Plenum Press.

Horowitz, M. J., Marmar, C., Krupnick, J., Wilner, N., Kaltreider, N., and Wallerstein, R. (1984). *Personality Styles and Brief Psychotherapy*. New York: Basic Books.

Horowitz, M. J., Marmar, C., Weiss, D., DeWitt, K., and Rosenbaum, R. (1984). Brief psychotherapy of bereavement reactions: the relationship of process to outcome. *Archives of General Psychiatry* 41:438–448.

Horowitz, M. J., Rosenbaum, R., and Wilner, N. (1988). Dilemmas of relationship: a new psychotherapy research process measure. *Psychotherapy: Theory, Research, Practice* 25:241–248.

Horowitz, M. J., and Zilberg, N. (1983). Regressive alterations in the self-concept. *American Journal of Psychiatry* 140(3): 284–289.

Kelly, G. A. (1955). *The Psychology of Personal Constructs*. New York: W. W. Norton.

Kernberg, O. (1975). *The Borderline Conditions and Pathological Narcissism*. New York: Jason Aronson.

Kiesler, D. J. (1979). An interpersonal communication analysis of relationship in psychotherapy. *Psychiatry* 42:299–311.

Kohut, H. (1977). *The Restoration of the Self*. New York: International Universities Press.

Langs, R. (1975). Therapeutic misalliances. *International Journal of Psychoanalytic Psychotherapy* 4:77–105.

Lubrosky, L., and Auerbach, A. H. (1985). The therapeutic relationship in psychodynamic psychotherapy: the research evidence and its meaning for practice. In *Psychiatry Update*, vol. 4, ed. A. J. Frances and R. E. Hales, pp. 550–572. Washington, DC: American Psychiatric Press.

Marmar, C., Marziali, E., Horowitz, M. J., and Weiss, D. (1986). The development of the therapeutic alliance rating system. In *Psychotherapeutic Process: A Research Handbook*, ed. L. Greenberg and W. Pinsoff. Philadelphia: Guilford Press.

Modell, A. H. (1976). The holding environment and the therapeutic action of psychoanalysis. *Journal of the Psychoanalytic Association* 24:285–308.

Myerson, P. (1977). Therapeutic dilemmas relevant to the lifting of repression. *International Journal of Psycho-Analysis* 58:458–463.

—— (1979). Issues of technique where patients relate with difficulty. *International Review of Psycho-Analysis* 6: 363–375.

Orlinsky, D. E., and Howard, K. (1975). *Varieties of Psychotherapeutic Experience*. New York: Teachers College Press.

Rosenbaum, R., Horowitz, M. J., and Wilner, N. (1986). Clinical assessment of patient difficulty. *Psychotherapy: Theory, Research, Practice* 23:417–425.

Ryle, A. (1975). *Frames and Cages.* New York: International Universities Press.

—— (1979). The focus in brief interpretive psychotherapy: dilemmas, traps, and snags as target problems. *British Journal of Psychiatry* 134:46–54.

Strupp, H. H. (1980a). Success and failure in time-limited psychotherapy, a systematic comparison of two cases: comparison one. *Archives of General Psychiatry* 37:595–603.

—— (1980b). Success and failure in time-limited psychotherapy, a systematic comparison of two cases: other comparisons. *Archives of General Psychiatry* 37:831–841, 941–954.

Winnicott, D. W. (1965). Ego distortion in terms of the true and false self. In *Natural Process and the Facilitating Environment.* New York: International Universities Press.

4

Visual Thought Images in Psychotherapy

One of the ground rules of psychotherapy is that the patient must attempt to put his thoughts and feelings into words and communicate them to the therapist. It has been noted, however, that many patients at times find they are unable to verbalize directly their ongoing psychic contents since mentation, instead of being formed in words, is being experienced as images of a sensory quality—usually visual. Such visual thought images lack the vividness, spatiality, and apparent reality of hallucinations or dreams, yet they may seem to enter consciousness fully formed and unbidden and may be difficult to dispel. The patient's verbal description of his imagoic cognition often yields rich stores of material highly relevant to his immediate motivational state, and the therapist will usually work with this in much the same way as he would with other imagery phenomena—dreams, hallucinations, screen memories, and so on. The occurrence of visual imagery in itself, aside from the actual image content, also conveys important information about the patient that is frequently overlooked. This chapter describes several situations in which visual thought images occur and clarifies the multiple functioning of such pictorializations.

The psychotherapeutic literature contains several references to the significance of the occurrence of a shift in cognitive modality from lexical to imagoic. Breuer and Freud (1895), in their work with such patients as Anna O., found visual images to be useful tools in gaining insight into the dynamics underlying the symptoms. Deutsch (1953) and Lewin (1955) noted that visual images arising in the course of associations during psychoanalysis function both as a resistance to verbalization and as a "furtherance" in terms of their communicative contents. Kanzer (1958) regards pictorializations as an intermediate state of consciousness between waking thought and dream formation; he notes that such alterations in consciousness occur when there is a feeling of shock following an interpretation. Warren (1961) found that a high frequency of visual imagery was reported when he asked patients what had entered their minds during periods in which there was a lapse in verbalization. On analysis, such visual images were seen to function as a transitory and uneasy resting place for conflict-laden instinctual impulses arising from the unconscious. Kepecs (1964) demonstrated that certain visual images were erected and used as a kind of screen or barrier against clear emergence of repressed material.

CLINICAL EXAMPLES

Three clinical examples are presented below to demonstrate the complexity of the dynamic issues and to stimulate the reader to recall his own professional experiences with visual thought images. The headings are of necessity oversimplified and indicate only one of the overdetermined functions of the imagery. No effort is made to present a complete dynamic discussion of the contents of the imagery.

Defensive Use of Visual Imagery

Here is an example of pictorialization of thought in which the imagery communicates thoughts and feelings which the patient wishes to remain unaware of but also is compelled to relate because of the wish to comply with the ground rules of treatment. As a compromise between resistance and compliance, a regressive form of mental representation is used.

A young woman in her 20s was being treated for a characterologic disturbance and had been in expressive psychotherapy for over one hundred hours. One day while entering, she imagined herself as being without her head and, after a silence, said she had nothing to talk about and that no thoughts would come to her. She then had a thought image of herself with a button on the side of her head. The button was pressed and letters, little white letters sorted into bundles, were emitted from her mouth. She then felt like an automaton and associated to people being laid off work because of "motivation," a slip of the tongue for "automation," and she laughed. Next she imaged a word game like Scrabble, and this was in the thought image of the game itself. Then she said, "That was like trying to sort words meaninglessly." The therapist stated that the slip "motivation" for "automation" might have something to do with her feelings about the therapy situation. The patient then continued to say that she felt treatment might be discontinued because of her apparent lack of motivation, and that this is what must have been meant by the thought image of entering without her head and automatically saying something to cover the fact that she felt she was holding back from the therapeutic process. Then she spoke more freely about an accident in which she had nearly been killed the previous week. She had not mentioned this during several previous hours of therapy. She discussed her feelings of resistance in therapy and began to work them through partially.

It is of interest that this same patient was able to alter her perceptual apparatus to achieve certain gratifying sensory effects. During a different therapy hour she found her attention focused on a brass book end, especially the handle. This book end, a part of the therapist's office, seemed to merge with her vision of the therapist's head (she was facing the therapist). Next she had a thought image of the book end striking the therapist's head. As she thought about these images, subsequent to having them as a sensory experience without any verbal insight into their meaning, she realized her irritation with the therapist because he had failed to congratulate or reward her in some way for some recent therapeutic progress. The therapist's "brass-headedness" seemed to be a connecting associative link between the thought image and the verbal, conceptual process. She then revealed her capacity to change the direction of gaze of a single eye which allowed her to move (in her internally perceived dyplopia) the book end toward and away from the therapist's head, since the book end was close enough that both were in the field of vision. She was thus capable of achieving a sensation of bashing in the therapist's head with the brass book end by control of her ocular muscles.

Defensive Use of Visual Imagery

Thought imges may be used to bolster the admonitions of the superego. This seems especially true when primitive superego introjects are present as internalized parental images. For example, a thought image of an angry and punitive parent may be used to bolster defenses against a repudiated impulse or even during acts of gratification.

A patient reported that during the penetration phase of sexual intercourse she regularly had the visual image of her mother staring at her with a frowning and reproving facial expression. This was accompanied by a momentary feeling of dread, which was shortly dispelled, as was the image. Neither this affect nor the repeated image interfered with gratification.

Certainly there are many other instances that arise in therapy of repeated visual images that accompany certain highly cathected or conflicted activities which seem to arise not only because of mnemonic and associative connections but fulfill some psychic purposes in the interplay between id, ego, and superego. The images, especially repetitive ones, are overdetermined and follow the principle of multiple functioning. In this case, for example, what was once a defense against impulse had become also a gratification of the impulse to "show her mother."

Enhancement of Visual Imagery with Failure in Regulation

A 43-year-old man had a pronounced obsessive-compulsive syndrome that occasionally was of psychotic proportions. His subjective experience of thinking was to find visual images forming in his "mind's eye" and then to fit appropriate words to the images for further thought and/or communication. When he was anxious, he was unable to convert these images into words and the images themselves would come in "flurries." At times almost all thought, imagoic and lexical, was blocked and the conscious contents of awareness were reported to consist of a repetitive, obsessive visual image of himself urinating. He stated that he could not prevent or remove this image by conscious effort but, paradoxically, he also found that having it seemed to reduce his anxiety. Prominent among his compulsions were frequent efforts to urinate, which were followed by a comparatively less anxious feeling of being "cleaned out and up-to-date." The act of urination and visualization of the act were symbolic condensations of many thought complexes, but associations of being purged of bad substances (for example, feces, evil intro-jects, bad thoughts, and unwholesome feelings) were common. These bad substances were out of control in other states of mind, including psychotic ones.

In his nonpsychotic states this patient was concerned to keep affect from consciousness. As a cognitive defense he scanned his visual imagery to expunge dangerous ideas or affects. Only after such a screening process could he allow representation of thought in words to develop. When motivational pressures and impaired regulatory capacities were such that conflicted material threatened to emerge, verbal cognition was entirely derailed and replaced with the obsessive visual image. By use of such rigid cognitive controls he was sometimes able to stabilize himself short of psychosis.

DISCUSSION

The three examples given illustrate that visual thought images are the result of unconscious thought processes that construct condensed, symbolic, visual representations of various motivational trends. Aside from the meaning of the imagoic contents, it is important to note in psychotherapy the process aspects of the occurrence of imagery, that is, in what situations does thought tend to shift from lexical to imagoic representation? This will differ from patient to patient and, within an individual, from one mental state to another. Some generalizations, however, can be attempted.

Clinical experience suggests that visual thought image reports tend to arise in the following situations:

1. When there is resistance to forming a lexical thought product, there may be a shift to nonlexical thought. This occurs when a patient wishes to avoid thinking clearly lest he become aware of thoughts that are anxiety-provoking. For some patients it seems possible to escape self-censure and the fear of communication by representing in visual images certain thoughts or feelings that, if conceived lexically, might give rise to anxiety.

2. Visual images may arise when the patient does not have immediately available to him the verbal facility to represent some experienced set of feelings or ideas. This state of groping unsuccessfully for suitable words occurs most often when ideas or feelings are just emerging into consciousness.

3. Memories that are preverbal, emotionally arousing, traumatic, highly meaningful, and/or partially screened from consciousness may first enter awareness as imagery and lose this sensory quality only when they are translated into lexical terms and the associated affect is worked through.

4. Imagery increases with regression in thinking, drowsiness, and altered states of consciousness. Mentation in the imagoic modality is not identical with primary process organization of thought, although they frequently occur simultaneously.

As indicated above, pictorialized thought may be part of a style of cognitive control or defense. Cognitive style is so widely variable that only a few of the more common usages of visual imagery will be remarked on here. In one style, affects are split off and isolated from ideas: one aspect, usually the affect, may be represented in imagery and the other aspect, ideas, represented in words. Closely related is a style in which one topic or subtopic is represented lexically, the other nonlexically. Some patients may use a very tricky sort of undoing mechanism: the "doing" is in one form of representation, the "undoing" in the other. The above cognitive styles are more common in persons with obsessional processes.

Hysterical processes sometimes are manifested in cognitive styles in which conscious verbal cognition is so blocked that ideas, impulses, and feelings in ongoing mentation are represented almost exclusively in imagery form. This mechanism is often successful in keeping from the patient's awareness the connotative aspects of his thought. A similar process is seen in certain borderline patients who seem deficient in their capacity to deperceptualize memory and thought, and experience their thoughts as series of vivid and, to them, unrelated images.

CONCLUSION

Visual images are reported from time to time by patients from all diagnostic categories. Even aside from their content, visual thought images may convey important information about the patient in terms of his cognitive dynamics. It is suggested that much can be gained by attending to the modality in which thought is represented and the contexts in which shifts in the modality of thought representation from lexical to imagoic occur. Some nuances of therapy technique involve a suggestion to make such shifts, as will be discussed in the next section.

REFERENCES

Breuer, J. and Freud, S. (1895). Studies on hysteria. *Standard Edition* 2:1–17.

Deutsch, F. (1953). Instinctual drives and intersensory perceptions during the analytic procedure. In *Drives, Affects, Behavior*, ed. R. M. Loewenstein, pp. 216–228. New York: International Universities Press.

Kanzer, M. (1958). Image formation during free association. *Psychoanalytic Quarterly* 27:465.

Kepecs, J. (1964). Observations on screens and barriers in the mind. *Psychoanalytic Quarterly* 23:62.

Lewin, B. D. (1955). Dream psychology and the analytic situation. *Psychoanalytic Quarterly* 24:169.

Warren, M. (1961). The significance of visual images. *Journal of the American Psychoanalytic Association* 9:504.

PART TWO

NUANCES OF INTERPRETATION

5

Visual Imagery
and
Defensive Processes

Image techniques have been widely used in different psychotherapies (Singer 1974). When therapists employ image techniques, they usually do so to alter the operation of defensive processes and promote expression of usually warded-off mental contents.

The rational use of such techniques should rest, ideally, on a theoretical model of the place of image formation in the spectrum of thought and the operation of defensive processes in relation to this modality. This chapter offers such a model. After outlining the model, I detail five types of image-formation inhibition and then describe both interpretive and directive interventions aimed at these inhibitions.

In the first era of psychoanalysis, interpretations were presentations to the patient of his or her own unconscious thoughts. Later, with the development of ego psychology, emphasis shifted to include the importance of interpreting defenses. As ego psychology continues to develop, interpretation aims not only at presentation of warded-off contents and at confrontation with defense but also at drawing the patient's attention to cognitive maneuvers by which the defenses are accomplished.

When there is adequate evidence and the time is right, a therapist tells a patient that he is not thinking about a specific topic and explains why he is afraid to do so. A cognitive interpretation extends such interventions. It tells the patient how he is going about *not thinking* the thought and shows him how he might think about the topic. After presenting a model of the place of images in thought, we will examine such cognitive interventions in relation to inhibitions of the image system. It is through these various types of inhibition of all representational modalities that repression is accomplished. By drawing attention to the *specific site of inhibition* one gives the patient a conscious choice to alter what has been, up to that point, an unconsciously determined avoidance.

IMAGE FORMATION AS A MODE OF REPRESENTATION

Modes available for the conscious expression of meanings include enactive, image, and lexical representations. In

ordinary wakeful thought, these modes blend richly; reflective awareness seldom distinguishes one from another. This
multimodal thought is symbolized, in Figure 5-1, as the
center of the sphere of attention. As the periphery is
approached, there is less blending, and one may be aware
that a train of thought is pictorial rather than verbal, is in
auditory images rather than subvocal speech, or is a flow of
word meanings without sensory qualities. Each mode has
its own special utility and organizational properties as elaborated in Table 5-1.

Enactive thought depicts information in the form of
trial actions, with minor tensing of muscles. The flow of
enactive thoughts may be reflected in micromomentary
gestures and facial expressions, and competing action tendencies may be recognized (Haggard and Isaacs 1966).

Image thought allows continued information processing after perception and, as in dreams and daydreams,
can lend a sensory configuration to emergent ideas and
feelings.

In lexical thought the essential ingredients are word
meanings and grammatical organization. Conceptualization, reasoning, and abstract generalization are most secure
in this mode.

Each mode is composed of subsystems. Enactive systems may be organized by functional activities such as
different work sets or sports. Image systems are divided by
sensory modes: auditory, visual, olfactory, gustatory, tac-
tile, and proprioceptive. The visual mode is the focus of this
paper. The lexical system may be organized by different
languages, each with a specific vocabulary and grammar.

When emergent ideas enter a system, the information
may then be translated from one mode to another (indi-

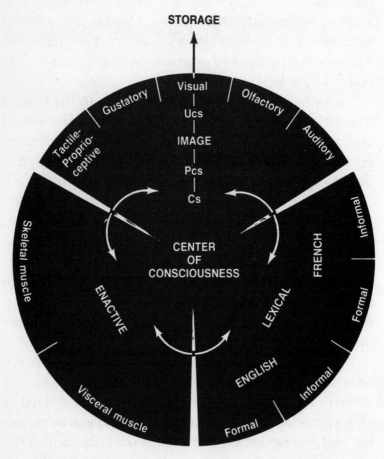

FIGURE 5-1   Modes of Conscious Representation

TABLE 5-1. An Outline of Modes of Representation

Enactive mode

Subsystems: Skeletal neuro-musculature. Visceral neuro-musculature.

Sample Organizational Tendencies: By directionality and force. By operational end-products.

Sample Statement: X does this.

Sample of Complex Units of Represented Information: Gestures. Facial expressions. Postures.

Image mode

Subsystems: Visual. Auditory. Tactile-kinesthetic. Olfactory-gustatory.

Sample Organizational Tendencies: By simultaneous occurrence. By spatial relationships. By concrete categorization of similarities and differences.

Sample Statements: X is like this. X is like Y. X is there and Y is there. X and Y happen together. X does this to Y.

Sample of Complex Units of Represented Information: Introjects. Body images. Relationship between self and object.

Lexical mode

Subsystems: Different languages.

Sample Organizational Tendencies: By sequentiality and linear structure. By abstract categorization.

Sample Statement: If X and Y then Z because X + Y → Z.

Sample of Complex Units of Represented Information: Phrases or sentences. Stories and histories.

cated by arrows in Figure 5-1). Regulatory processes act at the system boundaries to inhibit or facilitate these entries and exits.

UTILITY OF THE VISUAL IMAGE SYSTEM

Visual images are private experiences, rarely communicated by pictorialization, more often communicated by translation into words. Perhaps because of the early development of image formation, before conscientiousness or superego formation, or perhaps because of the privacy inherent in this mode, images often carry into awareness ideas censored from lexical representation. Such properties lead to the extremes of image use noted in clinical settings: At times the spontaneous flow of images seems almost like a direct expression of unconscious thought, as suggested by Freud (1900) and later by Jung (1916) in explanation of his active imagination technique. At times reversion to images is a withdrawal from verbal communication, a form of resistance (Kanzer 1958).

Images of dreams and waking fantasies often carry the first awareness of a newly emergent theme. Other clinical observations have shown that it is in this mode that preverbal memories (Kepecs 1954) and unresolved traumatic episodes may reenter awareness after a long period of repression (Horowitz 1986). Even if a theme has not initially gained entry into awareness in image form, the extension of ideas into image form is often associated with intensified emotion. Images can depict the intensity of a wish or fear because they reveal particular actions between persons. Finally, image experiences, even of entirely internal origin, may have a quasi-perceptual quality that allows the person a sense of interaction with them, on an as-if-real basis. Common examples are experiences of introjective presences and temporarily restorative fantasies of missing objects, from the fantasy of food in a starving person, to the fantasy of a separated lover, to the imaginary companion of a lonely child.

If these are the utilities of image representation, what motivates therapists to use interventions that increase image formation rather than those that encourage the continued employment of lexical thought? The most common aim is to short-circuit repression and elicit expression of warded-off ideas. The second most common aim is to short-circuit the partial repression involved in the more complex defenses of isolation and undoing and thus to uncover the emotion-arousing properties of thought.

Most frequently, the material then expressed in image form is composed of traumatic memories, conflicted interpersonal fantasies, and disavowed but dynamically powerful self-images. It is the conflict between current conscious attitudes and the wishes and fears inherent in these emergent images that generates emotional responses to the images experienced. This conflict can then, it is to be hoped, be worked through. As one step in working through such conflicts, image experiences are translated into word meanings. This extends awareness of meaning and alters the earlier state of censorship.

A MODEL OF THE IMAGE SYSTEM

Having described some of the properties of the image system, we may now consider a model of the system in order to focus on the possible sites for the accomplishment of defensive aims. Figure 5-2 provides a visual metaphor of such a model.

Stimuli enter the mind as information in the form of images. Eventually the information is transformed into the enactive and lexical forms suitable for usual interpersonal communication.

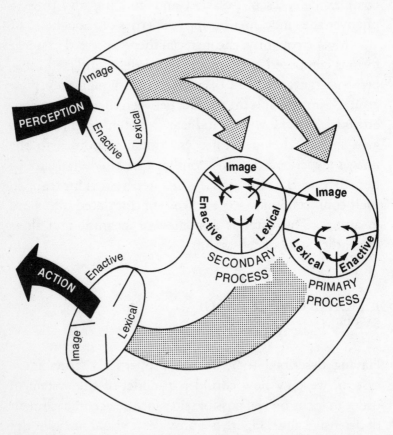

FIGURE 5-2 Transformations of Information in Perception, Conscious Representation, and the Media of Communication

For a time, the process of image thinking may take place in separable trains of thought, organized by relatively primary process, and also secondary process, regulations. The same stimulus situation is thus simultaneously contemplated in different ways. Comparison, and even competition, among these ways then occurs prior to any conclusive interpretation of a stimulus or decision on action.

Information enters the visual system from at least four and probably five sources, as shown in Figure 5-3. One source is perceptual input, including entoptic sensations. The second source is internal information, including both the schemata necessary to construct perceptual images and the storehouse of long-term memory and fantasy. The third input is from codings retained from prior episodes, episodes retained in a kind of short-term or active memory with a property of recurrent representation. The fourth input is translation from thought cycles occurring in other modes. The hypothetical fifth source is from parallel image-forming systems. Entry of information from a primary process type of image formation into a image system that has been regulated by secondary process is the instance of concern here. Defensive aims can be accomplished through the regulation of each of these forms of input.

DEFENSES AND THE PROCESS OF WORKING THROUGH

Working through involves, in part, the recognition and reconciliation of discrepancies between reality and fantasy, between current possibilities and inner attitudes or aims.

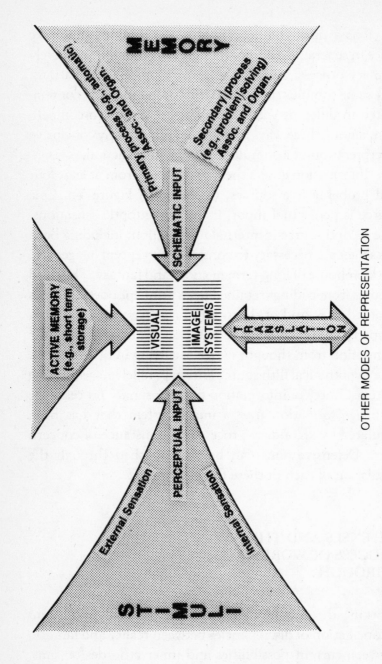

MEMORY

Primary process (e.g. "autonomic" Assoc. and Organ.)

Secondary/process (e.g. problem/solving) Assoc. and Organ.

SCHEMATIC INPUT

ACTIVE MEMORY (e.g. short term storage)

VISUAL IMAGE SYSTEMS

TRANSLATION

OTHER MODES OF REPRESENTATION

PERCEPTUAL INPUT

External Sensation

Internal Sensation

STIMULI

FIGURE 5-3 Input of Information from Diverse Sources into a Mode of Conscious Representation

Recognition and confrontation mean that ideas and feelings usually warded off are now expressed within a safe and therapeutic relationship. This process requires change in defensive operations and, generally, a change in the inhibitory maneuvers that accomplish repression. The model of representational modes presented here illustrates sites where inhibitions prevent the free flow of information in the form of visual images. One may now consider therapeutic interventions aimed at alteration of such inhibitions. The presence of a therapeutic relationship will be assumed.

TECHNIQUES TO ALTER
INHIBITORY OPERATIONS

The five most frequent inhibitions of entry of information into the visual image system are illustrated in Figure 5-4 as follows:

1. The failure to attach word labels to images.
2. The converse, which is avoidance of image associations to contents expressed in words.
3. Inattention to dim or fleeting image episodes.
4. The prevention of primary process or spontaneous flow types of image formation.
5. The nontranslation of enactive representations into imagery.

Overstated examples of interpretive and directive interventions are provided in Table 5-2 (Horowitz 1983). These are illustrative only. The directive remarks included

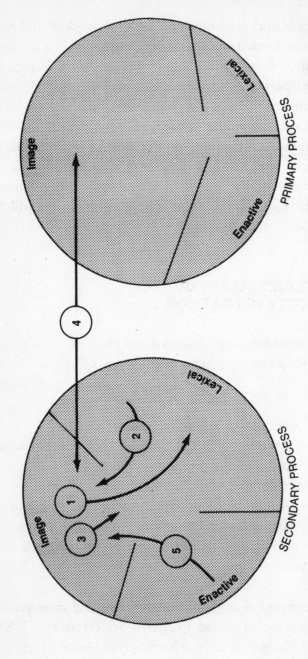

FIGURE 5-4 Locations in the Transformation of Information at which Inhibitions of a Potential Mental Content Might Occur (see text for explanation of the numbers)

TABLE 5-2. Defensive Inhibitions and Sample Interventions

Site of inhibition	Sample of an interpretive intervention	Sample of a directive intervention
Images not associated with word meanings	"You do not let yourself describe those images you are having because you are afraid to think clearly about and tell me about those ideas."	"Describe your images to me in words." "Tell me what that image means."
Lexical representations not translated into images	"You do not let yourself think that idea visually because you are afraid of the feelings that might occur if you did."	"Let yourself think in visual images and report whatever you experience to me."
Vague images (preconscious) not intensified (conscious)	"You are afraid to let that fleeting image become really clear in your mind because you are afraid you will feel or act badly if you do."	"Try to hold onto those images and 'tune them up.'"
No cross translation between secondary process and primary process images	"You are afraid to let yourself have day-dream images because you are afraid that bizarre ideas will take over and you will lose control."	"Let yourself kind of dream about this right now."
Enactive representations not translated into images	"You are afraid to picture in your mind the implications of your present posture and facial expression; you are afraid the self image that would result would shame you."	"Try to picture yourself in your mind with that posture and expression on your face."

in Table 5-2 are comparatively gentle in that they suggest to the patient changes in the form of thought. In guided fantasy techniques and behavior therapy techniques, direction is more extensive, and specific contents to conceptualize are suggested. The choice of interpretive or directive intervention for a given type of inhibition, as well as the timing, dosage, and nuances of intervention, is dependent on the current state of transference and the potential for transference topics—a subject too broad for discussion here.

Without going too far into the choice of interpretation or direction, what can be said about the difference between these techniques for the same type of inhibition? The directive interventions are similar to those of a teacher. If the assumption of a developmental lag is indicated, that is, if the patient has not yet learned to make full use of various modes of thought, if inhibition has been in fact a long-standing limitation of cognitive style, then a simple directive statement may help the patient learn new ways of using thought processes. Interpretive remarks are, of course, also covert suggestions. The patient hears such remarks as implications that he ought to try doing what he is told he is avoiding. But interpretive remarks give more information and so require more inference of knowledge on the part of the therapist. If this information is accurate and well timed, interpretations place the patient in a position of greater control. He can consciously choose to continue or to set aside the inhibitory processes set in motion by unconsciously made decisions.

The errors possible in intervention by direction or interpretation also influence the therapist's choice of technical style. Directive intervention, especially the suggestion of particular contents in guided fantasy techniques, may put the patient in a passive position; the directive acts of the therapist provide a nidus of reality for the elaboration of a transference in which the therapist is like a parent telling the patient what to do and holding him responsible as he complies or stubbornly resists in an overt or covert manner. Interpretive interventions can provide erroneous information that the patient may either believe or use against the therapist. For example, when the therapist interprets a behavior as defensive when it is in fact due to a lack of regulatory capacity, the interpretation does not help the patient gain control over his thought process.

FACILITATIONS AND INHIBITORY FAILURES

The avoidance of images can be contrasted with the intrusion of images. Episodes of unbidden images are more complex because they may result from either active facilitation or failure of inhibition. An example of interpretation of facilitated imagery follows. Suppose the patient becomes flooded with emotion because he has formed vivid images of a painful memory. The therapist might then interpret the transference: "You are upsetting yourself by forming lurid images of that event because you hope I will be compelled to comfort you if I see you cry." While this is an ordinary transference interpretation, albeit without a link to an earlier figure, it also conveys information about how cognitive processes are used. This is contained in the phrase "by forming lurid images." Such information puts the patient in a slightly better position to exert conscious choice over ensuing thought process.

Such an interpretation would be inappropriate if the main reasons for the lurid images were failures of inhibition. In this context, directive remarks might help the patient gain control. "Please contemplate that idea in words. You feel sad remembering this event. What did it mean to you?" At times, therapists suggest even more dramatic shifts to other modes as a way to learn control, as when Beck (1970) showed a patient with intrusive images that he could stop these images by clapping his hands.

It would also be possible for the therapist to direct attention to another topic, or to stay on the same topic but suggest specific images, as is done in behavior therapy techniques. For example, in systematic desensitization, the therapist takes phobic imagery, assembles a hierarchy of images from least to most threatening, and tells the patient when to start an image, what to image, and when to stop. This maneuver teaches the patient control over image formation; if the therapist can tell him to start and stop, he can tell himself the same thing.

MORE COMPLEX DEFENSIVE OPERATIONS

Defenses such as undoing and isolation are more complex than repression because they involve multiple cognitive operations. A brief clinical vignette provides an illustration of the play of such defenses at the boundaries of representational systems.

Early in a course of psychoanalytic psychotherapy, an obsessional man was describing a situation with his work supervisor and concealing from himself his hatred of this man.

The supervisor gave the patient more work than he thought he could do. As he tried to describe his response, he oscillated between feelings of respect and feelings of dislike for the way his supervisor told him to try to take on more work. In a given sentence, he would add undoing clauses: He admired the firmness of the supervisor, but he didn't like being given more work; he ought to do more, but it irritated him to be told to; he respected the supervisor, but the supervisor was too authoritarian; he spoke up to the supervisor, but in a wishy-washy way, and so forth.

The lexical system was the principal mode of representation here and lent itself to undoing because of its sequential organization. The therapist attempted to hold the patient to his irritation: Wasn't he saying that he did not like the supervisor when he gave him extra work?

The patient complained of the way the therapist said "did not like." That wording was too strong; sometimes he did admire the supervisor; at other times he felt less respect. The patient fell silent for a while, then reported the image of a door on which a red hot branding iron had just emblazoned an arrow. He could not think of what the image might mean, but felt vaguely frightened.

Reconsider the two states. In one the patient is thinking in words and communicating these mental contents. In the other, he has shifted to images, and for a time does not communicate. In the first state he manifests little emotion; in the second he reports feeling frightened. We know from other evidence that in both states he avoids clear depiction of himself as angry and destructive. In the lexical state he accomplishes this avoidance by using neutral words such as "respect" and "disrespect" and by changing his way of ascribing even these mild attitudes to himself. The requirements of grammar fix the subject and object as self or other: He respects or does not respect the supervisor.

In contrast, in the image system, the impulses are rather clear: The door is burned by the forcefully assertive branding iron. The patient avoids thinking of himself as angry by leaving the self and object designation unstated. Symbols are present—the door, the arrow, the iron, burning; but he does not identify himself with any of them. Instead he is frightened. In his kind of image thinking, his position as the subject or object of action can remain unclear; he is either the injured door, and hence frightened, or the out-of-control injuring iron, and hence frightened that he might hurt someone else.

As he translates the images into words and thinks of possible meanings related to himself, he can still accomplish undoing by verbal juggling—by changing ideas from self as victim to self as aggressor—which cancels anger by fear and fear by anger. The end result is, of course, only a vague sense of guilt and self-doubt.

To recapitulate, a given defensive aim, such as undoing, can be accomplished differently in different systems of representation. Some information leaks through to each system; subject and object are designated, but several oppositional interactions are asserted in order to maintain the protective confusion. In the image system, the emotional quality of the contemplated action is made clear, but the self-designation such as victim or aggressor is left unclear. The separation of the modes accomplishes isolation of idea from affect. The therapist, however, does not have to segregate information from either system; it is possible to pick up the emotional clues from the images, and the ideational clues from the words. Information derived from both states can be put together, the defensive codes broken, and the underlying threat recognized.

Intervention to help the patient set aside defenses in order to expose and deal with this threat will be a much longer process. It will involve interpretation of what is warded off, the manner of warding off, and the various cognitive maneuvers used to maintain defense. Change in cognitive style will involve the patient's learning to put together information by using both representational systems, just as the therapist has done.

CONCLUSION

There are several modes for the representation of thought. Thinking usually combines and orchestrates these modes. But each mode has a particular utility and is regulated in different ways. In particular states, especially in conflict when emergent ideas and feelings are avoided by defensive operations, the modes may be experienced as separable vehicles for expressing meanings. Defenses are accomplished by operations at the boundaries of each mode. An understanding of the cognitive process may help therapists choose interventions, either interpretive or directive, that are at the level of the patient's method of processing information. Such interventions may place a patient in a position of greater control, to the point that he can decide to experience thought in new ways—more consciously, expressively, and expansively.

REFERENCES

Beck, A. T. (1970). Role of fantasies in psychotherapy and psychopathology. *Journal of Nervous and Mental Diseases* 150:3–17.

Freud, S. (1900). The interpretation of dreams. *Standard Edition* 4/5:1–630.

Haggard, E. A., and Isaacs, K. S. (1966). Micromomentary facial expressions as indicators of ego mechanisms in psychotherapy. In *Methods of Research Psychotherapy*, ed. L. A. Gottschalk and A. H. Auerbach, pp. 154–165. New York: Appleton-Century-Crofts.

Horowitz, M. J. (1983). *Image Formation and Psychotherapy*. New York: Jason Aronson.

_____ (1986). *Stress Response Syndromes*. 2nd ed. Northvale, NJ: Jason Aronson.

Jung, C. G. (1916). *The Archetypes and the Collective Unconscious*. New York: Pantheon, 1959.

Kanzer, M. (1958). Image formation during free association. *Psychoanalytic Quarterly* 27:465–484.

Kepecs, J. G. (1954). Observations on screens and barriers in the mind. *Psychoanalytic Quarterly* 23:62–77.

Salzman, L. (1968). *The Obsessive Personality*. New York: Jason Aronson.

Singer, J. L. (1974). *Imagery and Daydream Methods in Psychotherapy and Behavior Modification*. New York: Academic Press.

6

Phase-Oriented Treatment of Stress Response Syndromes

In an earlier era the main treatments for traumatic neurosis involved either abreaction and catharsis or rest and emotional support. Yet there was no diagnostic category listed as "Traumatic Neurosis" in the official 1952 American Psychiatric Nomenclature (DSM-I) or in the 1968 revision (DSM-II). Posttraumatic stress disorders appeared only in DSM-III. Until then, neuroses that followed major external stress events were classified like

other types of neuroses according to presenting symptoms
or as "transient situational disturbances of adult life." On
the other hand, in the literature, in the courtroom, and in
conferences, the diagnosis "traumatic neurosis" was used
frequently, and there was considerable agreement on what
was meant by this term.

While posttraumatic hysteria had been noted by other
investigators (Veith 1965), Breuer and Freud (1893–1895)
were first to emphasize that physical traumas were less
important than psychic traumas in precipitating such
symptoms as recurrent visual hallucinations, emotional
attacks, and other sensory or motor disturbances. They
also noted that there was frequently a latent period between the occurrence of a stressful event and the onset of
symptoms.

Through elaborations and corrections of theory, the
concept of trauma became generalized; it was cited as
causative of various symptoms, conflicts, fixations, character traits, defenses, and adaptive and maladaptive cognitive and affective developments. The result was an array of
terms such as multiple traumas, strain traumas, cumulative
traumas, screen traumas, fantasy traumas, and retrospective traumas. In spite of this diffusion of terminology and
theory, the key findings remained quite clear to clinicians
and are consensually validated: After a traumatic event
there is a compulsive tendency toward mnemonic or symbolic repetition of some aspect of the experience (Freud
1920, Schur 1966).

The involuntary repetition of stress relevant information may stand in stark contrast to a seemingly opposite set
of responses: massive ideational denial of the event (or its
implications) and emotional numbness. Massive denial of

the stress event, or its implications, may alternate with intrusive repetitions in a variety of phasic relationships. A given time span in terms of hours or days may be characterized mainly by denial and numbness; it may alternate with phases of ideational intrusion and emotional pangs. At times, however, the two patterns may alternate in a shortened time span of seconds or minutes in length.

EPIDEMIOLOGICAL RESEARCH

Clinical studies are dependent on patients selected from usually unknown populations. Investigation of whole populations exposed to a variety of disasters and stresses obtains data on the generality of a phenomenon. The enormous populations exposed to the disasters of war in 1914-1918 and 1939-1945 not only confirmed but clarified many of the symptomatic responses noted in clinical investigations (Grinker and Spiegel 1945). One of the outcomes of experiences with reactions to combat was the expression "everyone has his breaking point." This slogan means that every person exposed to enough stress may show an acute stress response syndrome. Persons with certain latent neuroses or predispositions to certain stress-triggers may respond at lower levels of external stress, while persons with high stress tolerance will not "break down" until higher levels (Brill 1967).

Extended field studies also indicate that acute and chronic stress reactions do not have different constellations of symptoms and signs. In spite of efforts to distinguish different symptoms and signs of acute and chronic reactions (Kardiner and Spiegel 1947), the main difference is temporal onset or maintenance of the syndrome. This does not mean an absence of phasic changes, as will be discussed later, but simply that phases of symptoms and signs may occur in a short time after the stress event with apparent resolution (acute reactions), or they may persist for a long period or begin after a long latent period (chronic reactions).

Additional observational evidence arises from the most deplorable circumstances imaginable and indicates that profound and protracted stress may have chronic or permanent effects *no matter what the prestress personality.* This evidence is found in the decades of study of survivors of Nazi concentration camps. Study after study, as recently reviewed in two workshops (Krystal 1968, Krystal and Niederland 1971), confirms the occurrence of stress response syndromes, persistent for decades, in major proportions of those populations that survived protracted concentration camp experiences. As just one example, 99 percent of 226 survivors of a concentration camp in Norway had some psychiatric disturbance when intensively surveyed years after return to "normal life." Of the total population studied, 87 percent had cognitive disturbances such as poor memory and inability to concentrate, 85 percent had persistent nervousness and irritability, 60 percent had sleep disturbances, and 52 percent had nightmares (Eitinger 1969).

There seems little doubt, on the basis of these studies, that persons with *any* personality configuration before the stress will have symptoms such as recurrent unbidden images of camp experiences years after release. (This symptom, and the characteristic efforts to ward off intrusive thoughts, were dramatically portrayed in the film, *The Pawnbroker*.) Lifton (1967) has reported similar findings of chronic and permanent stress response symptoms or stress response types of personality damage in survivors of the atomic holocausts of Hiroshima and Nagasaki.

In clinical investigations, phasic repetition and denial have been emphasized. In field studies similar observations are noted (Bowlby and Parkes 1970, Davis 1966, Hamburg and Adams 1967). Once again a general response tendency appears to be visible through the variations imposed by differences in personality. Of course, all persons do not enter every phase, and they do not all go from one phase to the next in a fixed sequence or at the same time. But an overall patterned tendency can be abstracted from responses in a group of persons:

1. Phase of initial realization that a stress event has occurred (often with emotional "outcry").
2. Phase of denial and numbness.
3. Mixed phase of oscillation between denial with numbness and intrusive repetition in thought, emotional pangs, and/or compulsive-repetitive behaviors.
4. Phase of working through and acceptance, with loss of peremptory quality of either the denial or the recollection of stress event.

EXPERIMENTAL STUDIES

Clinical and field studies have scrutinized persons after the experience of major stress events. In the laboratory it is possible to control both subject selection and the quality of stressful stimuli. In a series of replicated studies of the effect of stress films on subsequent thought processes, Horowitz and Becker (1972) found that intrusive and repetitive thought occurred after this relatively mild or moderate level of stress and in a large proportion of various subject samples. These results provide additional support for the hypothesis that intrusive and repetitive thought is part of a general stress response syndrome that (1) may occur in varying intensity after various magnitudes of stress and (2) occurs in a broad spectrum of populations exposed to stress.

GENERAL STRESS RESPONSE SYNDROME

In psychoanalytic theory the phase of denial and numbness is conceptualized as the result of defensive overcontrol relative to an impulsive tendency to reexperience stressful events in thought and emotion. This defensive overcontrol wards off displeasure but prevents assimilation of the stressful event by association, averts appraisal of implications, and impedes working out plans of response. The phase of intrusive and repetitive thought and emotion is regarded as a defensive failure (undercontrol) even though the repetitions may, in the long run, reinitiate a working through process and lead to eventual mastery of the stress. The common symptoms of stress response syndromes can be categorized according to these two states (over- and undercontrol) as shown in Table 6-1.

In actual occurrence, the person might be in oscillation between overcontrol and undercontrol or in one state regarding a given ideational-emotional complex and another regarding a different ideational-emotional complex.

TABLE 6-1. Theoretical Organization of Common Stress Responses According to State of Control over Various Systems

Systems	States	
	Relative overcontrol	Relative undercontrol
Perception and attention systems	Blunting of perception and attention • daze • selective inattention	Hypervigilance, startle reactions
Conscious representation	Amnesia (complete or partial), nonexperience	Intrusive-repetitive thoughts and behaviors • illusions • pseudohallucinations • nightmares • reenactments, direct or symbolic • ruminations
Ideational processing systems (sequential and simultaneous organization of representations)	Denial, loss of reality appropriacy, constriction of associational width, inflexibility of organization of thought	Overgeneralization, inability to concentrate on other topics, preoccupation, confusion and disorganization
Emotional systems	Numbness	Emotional attacks or "pangs" (fear, guilt, rage, shame, sorrow)
Somatic systems	Tension-inhibition type symptoms	Symptomatic sequelae of chronic fight or flight readiness (or other exhaustion of such responses)
Control systems	If direct controls are insufficient, other control systems may be activated, leading to such symptoms as withdrawal, substitute or counterphobic behaviors, alteration of state of consciousness, or regression	

TREATMENT

In the past, there has been a tendency to determine treatment techniques by schools or "brand names." For example, psychoanalytically oriented psychiatrists in World War II tended toward *abreactive-cathartic treatments* and so-called "directive-organic" types tended toward *sedation, support, and rest.* Combinations of treatment were used by many, of course, and treatment was generally revised in the Korean and Vietnamese wars.

The central aims of the two broad categories of treatment can be stated at a very general level. Suppose the same person goes through phases of response after a stress event. These phases are determined, to a large extent, by the current degree of control over a tendency to repetition. In general, the rest and support type of treatments are efforts to supplement relatively weak controls. The treatment staff takes over some aspects of control operations, and they reduce the likelihood of emotional and ideational triggers to repeated representations. In contrast, the abreactive-cathartic methods reduce controls through suggestion, social pressure, hypnosis, or hypnotic drugs. The long-range goal of the abreactive-cathartic treatment is not to reduce controls, however, but to reduce the *need* for controls by helping the patient to complete the cycle of ideational and emotional responses to a stress event.

Such generalities orient understanding but do not help in the prescription of person-specific treatments. Any individual treatment is constructed by selection of many specific maneuvers from the repertoire of available techniques. This selection is based upon clinical inference about the patient's immediate state and guided by theory. Unfortunately the contemporary repertoire of available techniques is poorly classified, especially with reference to the treatment of stress reactions. Many different techniques have been advocated (Solomon et al. 1971), but they have not been theoretically or empirically compared in any systematic way. A review of the literature has led me to list treatment techniques advocated at one time or another according to the same format used to classify the stress response symptoms. The result is Table 6-2. Once again, the basic situation is conceptualized as a strong impulsive tendency toward repetition until completion, a tendency opposed by defenses and controls that vary in strength and capacity. The vertical columns delineate over- and under-control. The rows describe gross separations of systems of control, information, and emotional processing. The treatments are grouped at the intersection of row and column because they are conceptualized as attempts to alter *that* state of *that* system.

Please note that Table 6-2 is not an attempt to advocate any particular treatment. Techniques from various schools are included (for instance, interpretation of unconscious dynamic configurations, moral persuasion, biofeedback, desensitization), in an attempt to organize many empirically derived approaches into a common theoretical framework. Whether a given technique *works* or not is not the topic; what it *aims* at doing is the topic. Obviously the listing is not exhaustive (see Horowitz 1986).

PHASES AND PRIORITIES OF TREATMENT

In the course of an overall treatment, several alterations in technique would be indicated as phases shifted. The first

TABLE 6-2.   Treatments for Stress Response Syndromes

States	
Denial-numbing phase	Intrusive-repetitive phase
Reduce controls • interpret defenses and attitudes that make controls necessary • suggest recollection	Supply structure externally • structure time and events for patient when essential • organize information Reduce external demands and stimulus levels Rest Provide identification models, group membership, good leadership, orienting values Permit temporary idealization, dependency
Encourage abreaction Encourage description • association • speech • use of images rather than just words in recollection and fantasy • conceptual enactments, possibly also role playing and art therapy Reconstructions to prime memory and associations Encourage catharsis Explore emotional aspects of relationships and experiences of self during event Supply support and encourage emotional relationships to counteract numbness	Work through and reorganize by clarifying and educative interpretive work Differentiate • reality from fantasy • past from current schemata • self-attributes from object attributes Remove environmental reminders and triggers, interpret their meaning and effect Teach "dosing," e.g., attention on and away from stress-related information Support Evoke other emotions, e.g., benevolent environment Suppress emotion, e.g., selective use of antianxiety agents Desensitization procedures and relaxation

priority would be termination of the impact of the external stress event on the patient. If it is assumed that this can be and has been done, the second priority is to help reduce the amplitude of oscillations of thought and affective response to tolerable levels. Increasing the patient's toleration, as with support, is one means to this end, but there are many other techniques listed under "states of undercontrol."

Once a swing from relative denial to relative recollection and association can be tolerable to the patient, the next (third) priority may be to encourage such oscillations. In other words, the therapist would help the patient "dose" the periods of realization and cognitive-affective response within limits of toleration, using techniques from either category as indicated to start or stop the process. Then, the fourth priority is to help the patient work through the reactivated experience in terms of detailed and varied conceptual and emotional responses. These priorities of treatment are summarized in Table 6-3.

CONCLUSION

In a complex clinical situation the concept of phases can be applied to differing sectors of response. After a stress event a patient may be in a state of intrusive and repetitive thinking about one set of meanings and in a phase of denial and numbness for another set of meanings. For example, after death of a spouse, a patient may have repetitive-intrusive ideas and pangs of guilt over hostile attitudes toward the spouse, but deny and ward off sadness and ideas related to the object loss. In the conduct of psychotherapy, the therapist may regard the former set of ideas and emotions as in a state of relative undercontrol, and the latter set

TABLE 6-3. Priorities of Treatment

Patient's current state	Treatment Goal
Under continuing impact of external stress event.	• Terminate external event or remove patient from contiguity with it. • Provide temporary relationship. • Help with decisions, plans, or working through.
Swings to intolerable levels: • Ideational-emotional attacks. • Paralyzing denial and numbness	• Reduce amplitude of oscillations to swings of tolerable intensity of ideation and emotion. • Continue emotional and ideational support.
Frozen in overcontrol state of denial and numbness with or without intrusive repetitions.	• Help patient "dose" reexperience of event and implications by techniques that help him remember for a time, put out of mind for a time, remember for a time, and so on. • During periods of recollection, help patient organize and express experience. Increase sense of safety in therapeutic relationship so patient can resume processing the event.
Able to experience and tolerate episodes of ideation and waves of emotion.	• Help patient work through associations: the conceptual, emotional, object relations, and self-image implications of the stress event. • Help patient relate this stress event to earlier threats, relationship models, self-concepts, and future plans.
Able to work through ideas and emotions on one's own.	• Work through loss of therapeutic relationship. • Terminate treatment.

of ideas and emotions (if inferred) as in a state of relative overcontrol. This oversimplified example is meant only to indicate that the "complexes" of a given patient may each have their own phases and priorities, with differing treatment techniques applicable to each.

REFERENCES

Bowlby, J., and Parkes, C. M. (1970). Separation and loss. In *International Yearbook of Child Psychiatry and Allied Disciplines*, vol. 1, *The Child in his Family*, ed. E. Anthony and C. Koupernik, pp. 197–217. New York: Wiley.

Breuer, J., and Freud, S. (1893–1895). Studies on hysteria. *Standard Edition* 2:1–17.

Brill, N. G. (1967). Gross stress reactions. II. Traumatic war neuroses. In *Comprehensive Textbook of Psychiatry*, ed. A. M. Freedman and H. I. Kaplan, pp. 1031–1035. Baltimore: Williams and Wilkins.

Coelho, G. V., Hamburg, D. A., and Adams, E. (1970). *Coping and Adaptation. A Behavioral Sciences Bibliography*. Washington, DC: Public Health Service Publication #2087.

Davis, D. R. (1966). *An Introduction to Psychopathology*. London: Oxford University Press.

Eitinger, L. (1969). Psychosomatic problems in concentration camp survivors. *Journal of Psychosomatic Research* 13:183.

Freud, S. (1920). Beyond the pleasure principle. *Standard Edition* 18:1–68.

Furst, S. S. (1967). *Psychic Trauma: A Survey*. New York: Basic Books.

Grinker, R., and Spiegel, J. (1945). *Men Under Stress*. Philadelphia: Blakiston.

Hamburg, D. A., and Adams, J. E. (1967). A perspective on coping behavior. *Archives of General Psychiatry* 17:277.

Horowitz, M. J. (1986). *Stress Response Syndromes*. Northvale, NJ: Jason Aronson.

Horowitz, M. J., and Becker, S. S. (1972). Cognitive response to stress: experimental studies of a compulsion to repeat trauma. *Psychoanalytic Contemporary Science* 1:258.

Janis, I. L. (1958). *Psychological Stress: Psychoanalytic and Behavioral Studies of Surgical Patients.* New York: Wiley.

Kardiner, A., and Spiegel, H. (1947). *War Stress and Neurotic Illness.* New York: Hoeber Medical Division, Harper & Row.

Krystal, H. (1968). *Massive Psychic Trauma.* New York: International Universities Press.

Lazarus, R. S. (1966). *Psychological Stress and the Coping Process.* New York: McGraw-Hill.

Lifton, J. R. (1967). *History and Human Survival.* New York: Vintage Books.

Niederland, W. G. (1968). Clinical observations on the "survivor syndrome." *International Journal of Psychiatry* 49:313.

Schur, M. (1966). *The Id and the Regulatory Principles of Mental Functioning.* New York: International Universities Press.

Selye, H. (1936). A syndrome produced by diverse nocuous agents. *Nature* 138:32.

Solomon, G. F., Zarcone, Jr., V. P., Yoerg, R., Scott, N. R., and Maurer, R. G. (1971). Three psychiatric casualties from Vietnam. *Archives of General Psychiatry* 25:522.

Veith, I. (1965). *Hysteria of a Disease.* Chicago: University of Chicago Press.

7

Character Style in Stress Response Syndromes

Stress response syndromes are the topic, but the larger aim of this chapter is to test a model for organizing clinical knowledge. The model integrates variables that characterize current state, personal style, and treatment technique. To reduce information to a coherent level, particular categories along each dimension are designated. The interactions are then examined. Here, a particular domain is circumscribed by state in terms of stress response syndromes, disposition in terms of compulsive and histrionic personality, and by treatment in terms of focal psychodynamic psychotherapy. If this model works for circumscribing a domain and assembling assertions within it, then it can be used with other states, styles, and treatments. The resulting organization of clinical knowledge would allow a clear focus for resolution of disputes about observation and therapy.

RATIONALE FOR CHOICES

State: Stress Response Syndromes

Stress response syndromes have been chosen because the general symptomatic tendencies are well documented, observed across various populations, and usually change rapidly during psychotherapy. External stress events are usually clear and provide the therapist with a point of reference for consideration of other material.

Disposition: Histrionic and Compulsive Neurotic Styles

Compulsive and histrionic styles are classical typologies in dynamic psychology. Theorization about these styles is at the same level of abstraction as theories of stress, in that both stress response syndromes and obsessional and hysterical styles have been described in terms of potentially conscious cognitive and emotional processes. Information processing theory will thus provide a useful language.

Technique: Time-limited Psychodynamic Therapy for Stress Response Syndromes

The goals of psychotherapy are infinite. Here they will be limited to conceptual and emotional working through of the stress response syndrome to a point of relative mastery, a state in which both denial and compulsive repetition are reduced or absent.

Nuances of techniques such as repetition, clarification, and interpretation will be focused on, since these maneuvers are on an information processing level of abstraction. The nature of the relationship between patient and therapist will also be examined, but the complexities of transference and resistance will not be discussed in detail.

The basic knowledge relevant to each choice will now be summarized and followed by development of their interactions.

The Natural Course of Stress Response Syndromes

Multiple meanings confound the use of the word "stress." In psychiatry, the central application is concerned with the stress event that triggers internal responses and evokes potentially disruptive quantities or qualities of information and energy. A prototype of a stress event is a highway accident; an elaboration of this prototype will be used to provide a concrete reference for what follows.

Before we develop this example, some reminders set the stage. Freud and Breuer (1893–1895) found that traumatic events were repressed and yet involuntarily repeated in the form of hysterical symptoms. While some "reminiscences" of their hysterical patients stemmed more from fantasy than from reality, the central observation of compulsive repetition of trauma was validated in many later clinical, field, and experimental studies (Freud 1920, Furst 1967, Grinker and Spiegel 1945, Horowitz and Becker 1972). A second common set of stress responses includes ideational denial and emotional numbing. These signs seem antithetical to intrusive repetitions and are regarded as a defensive response (Hamburg and Adams 1967, Horowitz 1973, Lifton 1967). Tendencies to both intrusive repetition and denial-numbing occur in populations that vary in predisposition, after stressful events that vary in intensity and quality, and may occur simultaneously in a given person or in patterns of phasic alteration.

There is a common pattern to the progression of phases of stress response. With the onset of the stress event, especially if it is sudden and unanticipated, there may be emotional reactions, such as crying out or a stunned, uncomprehending daze. After these first emotional reactions and physical responses, as described in the preceding chapter, there may be a period of comparative denial and numbing. Then an oscillatory period commonly emerges in which there are episodes of intrusive ideas or images, attacks of emotion, or compulsive behaviors alternating with continued denial, numbing, and other indications of efforts to ward off the implications of the new information. Finally, a phase of "working through" may occur in which there are less intrusive thoughts and less uncontrolled attacks of emotion with greater recognition, conceptualization, stability of mood, and acceptance of the meanings of the event (Bowlby and Parks 1970, Davis 1966, Horowitz 1973, Janis 1969, Lazarus 1966).

THEORY OF PSYCHIC TRAUMA

Freud's theories about trauma have two important aspects: the neurotic and energic definitions of traumatization. In early theory, a traumatic event was defined as such because it was followed by neurotic symptoms. To avoid circularity, a theoretical explanation of traumatization was necessary. The energic explanation defined as traumatic those events that led to excessive incursions of stimuli. In a series of energy metaphors, stimuli from the outer world were postulated to exceed a "stimulus barrier" or "protective shield." The ego tried to restore homeostasis by "discharging," "binding," or "abreacting" the energy. Energy, instinctual drives, and emotions were often conceptually blended together in this model.

While Freud repeated energy metaphors throughout his writings, he also conceptualized trauma in cognitive terms more compatible with contemporary psychodynamic models. As early as 1893 in his lecture "On the Psychical Mechanism of Hysterical Phenomena," he spoke of how one could deal with the affect of a psychic trauma by working it over associatively and producing contrasting ideas (Freud 1893). Also implicit in his formulations of signal anxiety is the concept of ideational appraisal of events and their implications (Freud 1926).

The concept of information overload can be substituted for excitation or energy overload (Appelgarth 1971, Horowitz and Becker 1972). Information applies to ideas of inner and outer origin as well as to affects. The persons remain in a state of stress or are vulnerable to recurrent states of stress until this information is processed. It is the information that is both repressed and compulsively repeated until processing is relatively complete. Emotions, which play such an important part in stress response syndromes, are not seen as drive or excitation derivatives, but as responses to ideational incongruities and as motives for defense, control, and coping behavior. This view of the centrality of ideational processing is consistent with French's conceptualization of integrative fields (French 1952) and the concept of emotion with ideational incongruities is concordant with cognitive formulations of emotion (Lazarus et al. 1970) and cognitive-neurophysiological formulations (Pribham 1967).

Prototypic Example

These generalizations will be given concrete reference in the form of a story. The story is intended as a prototype and will be elaborated in various ways as an exercise. That is, the story will allow a hypothetical constancy of events and problems but a variation in personality style. We shall imagine this story as if it happened to two persons, one with a hysterical neurotic style, the other with an obsessional style. Thus, similar response tendencies to the same stress event can be contrasted in terms of stylistic variations and the nuances of treatment applicable to these variations.

Harry is a 40-year-old truck dispatcher. He had worked his way up in a small trucking firm. One night he himself took a run because he was short-handed. The load was steel pipes carried in an old truck. This improper vehicle had armor between the load bed and the driver's side of the forward compartment but did not fully protect the passenger's side.

Late at night Harry passed an attractive and solitary girl hitchhiking on a lonely stretch of highway. Making an impulsive decision to violate the company rule against passengers of any sort, he picked her up on the grounds that she was a hippie who did not know any better and might be raped.

A short time later, a car veered across the divider line and entered his lane, threatening a head-on collision. He pulled over the shoulder of the road into an initially clear area, but crashed abruptly into a pile of gravel. The pipes shifted, penetrated the cab of the truck on the passenger's side, and impaled the girl. Harry crashed into the steering wheel and windshield and was briefly unconscious. He regained consciousness and was met with the grisly sight of his dead companion.

The highway patrol found no identification on the girl; the other car had driven on, and Harry was taken by ambulance to a hospital emergency room. No fractures were found; his lacerations were sutured, and he remained overnight for observation. His wife, who sat with him, found him anxious and dazed that night, talking episodically of the events in a fragmentary and incoherent way so that the story was not clear.

The next day he was released. Against his doctor's

recommendations for rest and his wife's wishes, he returned to work. From then on, for several days, he continued his regular work as if nothing had happened. There was an immediate session with his superiors and with legal advisors. The result was that he was reprimanded for breaking the rule about passengers but also reassured that, otherwise, the accident was not his fault and he would not be held responsible. As it happened, the no-passenger rule was frequently breached by other drivers, and this was well known throughout the group.

During this phase of relative denial and numbing, Harry thought about the accident from time to time but was surprised to find how little emotional effect it seemed to have. He was responsible and well-ordered in his work, but his wife reported that he thrashed around in his sleep, ground his teeth, and seemed more tense and irritable than usual.

Four weeks after the accident he had a nightmare in which mangled bodies appeared. He awoke in an anxiety attack. Throughout the following days, he had recurrent, intense, and intrusive images of the girl's body. These images together with ruminations about the girl were accompanied by anxiety attacks of growing severity. He developed a phobia about driving to and from work. His regular habits of weekend drinking increased to nightly use of growing quantities of alcohol. He had temper outbursts over minor frustrations and experienced difficulty concentrating at work and even while watching television.

Harry tried unsuccessfully to dispel his ruminations about feeling guilty for the accident. Worried over Harry's complaints of insomnia, irritability, and increased alcohol consumption, his doctor referred him for psychiatric treatment. This phase illustrates the period of compulsive repetition in waking and dreaming thought and emotion.

Harry was initially resistant, in psychiatric evaluation, to reporting the details of the accident. This resistance subsided relatively quickly and he reported recurrent intrusive images of the girl's body. During the subsequent course of psychotherapy, Harry worked through several complexes of ideas and feelings linked associatively to the accident and his intrusive images. The emergent conflictual themes included guilt over causing the girl's death, guilt over the sexual ideas he fantasied about her before the accident, guilt that he felt glad to be alive when she had died, and fear and anger that he had been involved in an accident and her death. To a mild extent, there was also a magical or primary process belief that the girl "caused" the accident by her hitchhiking, and associated anger with her, which then fed back into his various guilt feelings.

EXPLANATORY THEORY

Before continuing with those conflicts triggered by the accident, it is helpful to consider, at a theoretical level, the ideal route of conceptualization that Harry should follow. To reach a point of adaptation to this disaster, Harry should perceive the event correctly; translate these perceptions into clear meanings; relate these meanings to his enduring attitudes; decide on appropriate actions; and revise his memory, attitude, and belief systems to fit this new development in his life. During this information processing, Harry should not ward off implications of the event or relevant associations to the event. To do so would impair his capacity to understand and adapt to new realities.

Human thought does not follow this ideal course. The accident has many meanings sharply incongruent with Harry's previous world picture. The threat to himself, the possibility that he has done harm, the horrors of death and injury, and the fear of accusation by others seriously differ from his wishes for personal integrity, his current self-images, and his view of his life role. This dichotomy between new and old concepts arouses strong painful emotions that threaten to flood his awareness. To avoid such unbearable feelings, Harry limited the processes of elaborating both "real" and "fantasy" meanings of the stressful event.

Because of complex meanings and defensive motives that impede conceptualization, the traumatic perceptions are not rapidly processed and integrated. They are stored because they are too important to forget. The storage is in an active form of memory that, hypothetically, has a tendency toward repeated representation. This tendency triggers involuntary recollections until processing is completed. On completion, the stored images are erased from active memory (Horowitz 1986, Horowitz and Becker 1972). (This memory is called "active" rather than "short-term" because of the extended duration of intrusive repetitions of stress-related perceptions.) The repetitions, however intrusive, can be adaptive when they provoke resumption of processing. They can be maladaptive when they distract from other tasks, elicit painful emotions, evoke fear of loss of mental control, and motivate pathological defenses.

Defensive operations that oppose repetition can also

be adaptive because they allow gradual assimilation rather than overwhelming recognition. Defense maneuvers can be maladaptive if they prevent assimilation, lead to unrealistic appraisals, perpetuate the stress response symptoms, or lead to other problems, such as Harry's alcoholism.

The six problematic themes of Harry's psychotherapy can now be reconsidered as ideational-emotional structures in schematic form. These themes will provide a concrete referent during the ensuing discussion of character style variations. In Table 7-1, each theme is represented as a match between a current concept and enduring concepts. Since there is an incongruity between the new and the old, the elicited emotion is also listed.

Three themes cluster under the general idea that Harry sees himself as an aggressor and the girl as a victim. For example, he felt relief that he was alive when someone "had to die." The recollection of this idea elicited guilt because it is discrepant with social morality. He also felt as if he were the aggressor who caused a victim to die because of his wish to live, a primitive concept that someone has to die, and a belief in the magical power of his thought. Similarly, his sexual ideas about the girl before the crash were recalled and were incongruent with his sense of sexual morality and marital fidelity. All three themes are associated with guilty feelings.

Three other themes center around an opposite conceptualization of himself, this time as a victim. Harry is appalled by the damage to the girl's body. It means his body could also be damaged. This forceful idea interferes with his usual denial of personal vulnerability, and is inconsistent with wishes for invulnerability. The result is fear. Harry also conceives of himself as a victim when he recalls that he

TABLE 7-1. Themes Activated by the Accident

Current concept — Incongruent with — "Enduring" concept → Emotion		
A. Self as "aggressor"		
A1. Relief that she and not he was the victim	Social morality	Guilt
A2. Aggressive ideas about girl	Social morality	Guilt
A3. Sexual ideas about girl	Social morality	Guilt
B. Self as "victim"		
B1. Damage to her body could have happened to him	Invulnerable self	Fear
B2. He broke rules	Responsibility to company	Fear (of accusations)
B3. She instigated the situation by hitchhiking	He is innocent of any badness; the fault is outside	Anger

broke company rules by picking up a passenger. Since the breach resulted in a disaster, and is discrepant with his sense of what the company wants, he believes accusations would be justified and is frightened. "Harrys" with varying character styles would experience this same theme in different ways. A Harry with a paranoid style might project the accusation theme and suspect that others are now accusing him. He might use such externalizations to make himself feel enraged rather than guilty. If Harry had a histrionic style, he might have uncontrolled experiences of dread or anxiety without clear representation of the instigating ideas. Were he compulsive, Harry might ruminate about the rules; about whether they were right or wrong, whether he had or had not done his duty, about what he ought to do next, and on and on.

The last theme cited in Table 7-1 places Harry as a victim of the girls' aggression. His current ideas are that she made the disaster happen by appearing on the highway. This matches with his enduring concept of personal innocence in a way that evokes anger. These angry feelings are then represented as a current concept and responses occur to these concepts that again transform Harry's state. His felt experience of anger and his concept of the girl as aggressor do not mesh with his sense of reality. The accident was not her fault and so, as the state of ideas change, his emotional experience (or potential emotional experience) changes. He feels guilty for having irrational and hostile thoughts about her. With this switch from the feelings of victim to the feelings of aggressor, there has been a change in emotions from anger to guilt and, as diagrammed in Table 7-1, in state from B3 to A2.

All six themes might be activated by the accident. In "Harrys" of different neurotic character styles, some themes might be more important or conflictual than others. In a hysterical Harry, sexual guilt themes (A3) might predominate. In an obsessional Harry, aggression-guilt (A2), concern for duty (B2), and "self as an innocent victim" themes (B3) might predominate. Other themes, such as fear of body vulnerability (B1) and guilt over being a survivor (A1) seem to occur universally (Furst 1967, Lifton 1967).

Harry had a period in which there was relative denial and numbness for all the themes. Later, at various times after the accident, some themes were repressed and others emerged; eventually some were worked through so that they no longer aroused intense emotion or motivated defensive efforts. The first emergent themes were triggered by the nightmare of mangled bodies and the daytime recurrent unbidden images of the girl's body. The themes of bodily injury and survivor guilt (A1 and B1) were no longer completely warded off but rather occurred in an oscillatory fashion with periods of both intrusion and relatively successful inhibition. In psychotherapy, these intrusive themes required first attention. The other themes such as sexual guilt emerged later.

GENERAL STRATEGEMS OF TREATMENT FOR STRESS RESPONSE SYNDROMES

At least two vectors affect stress response syndromes: the tendencies to repeated representation and the tendencies to inhibited representation to prevent disruptive emotions. The general rationale of treatment is to prevent either extreme denial, which might impede conceptual and emotional processing, or extreme intrusive-repetitiousness, which might cause panic states or secondary avoidance maneuvers.

Once extreme symptoms are reduced, the task is to bring stress-related information to a point of completion. This "completion" can be defined, at the theoretical level, as a reduction of the discrepancy between current concepts and enduring schemata. The crucial feature is not discharge of pent-up excitation, as suggested by the terms "abreaction" and "catharsis," but processing of ideas. To complete the response cycle, either new information must be reappraised or previous concepts must be modified to fit an altered life. Emotional responses will occur during this process when conflicts of meanings are fully considered.

Investigation, in focal psychodynamic treatment, includes examination of conflicts present before and heightened by the immediate situation, as well as the loaded meanings given to stressful events because of prior development experiences and fantasies. Conscious representation is encouraged because it promotes the solving of problems not resolved by automatic, out-of-awareness thought or dreaming. The communicative situation encourages representation and reexamination, and techniques of repetition, clarification, and interpretation enhance the ongoing process (Bibring 1954).

The state of stress imposed by a particular life event may impose a general regression in which developmentally primitive adaptive patterns will be noted, latent conflicts will be activated and more apparent, and increased demand for parental objects will affect all interpersonal relationships. These general regressive signs will subside without specific therapeutic attention, if the state of stress is reduced by working through the personal meanings of the particular life event.

The problem in therapy is to provide tolerable doses of awareness because knowledge of the discrepancies between desire and reality leads to painful emotional responses. On his own, the patient has warded off such knowledge to avoid pain and uncertainty. In therapy, while the affective responses are painful, they are held within bearable limits because the therapeutic relationship increases the patient's sense of safety (Greenson 1965). In addition, the therapist actively and selectively counters defensive operations by various kinds of intervention. These interventions are, most commonly, clarification and interpretation of specific memories, fantasies, and impulse-defense configurations.

The aim of these techniques is completion of ideational and emotional processing and hence, resolution of stress state rather than extensive modification of character. However, persons of different character structure will manifest different types of resistance and transference during this process. The general techniques will be used with various nuances depending on these dispositional qualities of the patient. As illustration, histrionic and compulsive variations on these general themes will now be considered.

HISTRIONIC STYLE IN RESPONSE TO STRESS

Background

The concept of what was first called hysterical character was developed in the context of psychoanalytic studies of hysterical neuroses, even though these neuroses may occur in persons without hysterical character and persons with hysterical styles do not necessarily develop hysterical neurotic symptoms, even under stress. The discussion will briefly develop the "ideal" typology of histrionic style with the assumption that most persons will have only some of the traits and no person will fit the stereotype perfectly. I use the terms *hysterical* and *histrionic* interchangeably.

The main symptoms of hysterical neuroses are either conversion reactions or dissociative episodes (Janet 1965). Both symptom sets have been related to dynamically powerful but repressed ideas and emotions that would be intolerable if they gained conscious expression (Freud and Breuer 1893–1895, Freud 1893). In classical analytic theory, the intolerable ideas are a wish for a symbolically incestuous love object. The desire is discrepant with moral standards and so elicits guilt and fear. To avoid these emotions, the ideational and emotional cluster is warded off from awareness by repression and denial. Because the forbidden ideas and feelings press for expression, there are continuous threats, occasional symbolic or direct breakthroughs, and a propensity for traumatization by relevant external situations. While later theorists have added the importance of strivings for dependency and attention ("oral" needs), rage over the frustration of these desires, and the fusion of these strivings with erotic meanings, the correlation of hysterical symptoms with efforts at repression remained an emphasis (Easser and Lesset 1965, Ludwig 1972, Marmor 1953).

Since the modern term is *histrionic*, it will be used as synonymous with the classical *hysterical*. Psychoanalysts view histrionic personality as typically exhibitionistic, labile in mood, and prone to act out.

Because of a proclivity for acting out oedipal fantasies, clinical studies suggest that such persons are more than usually susceptible to stress response syndromes after seductions, especially those that are sadomasochistic; after a loss of persons or of positions that provided direct or symbolic attention or love; after a loss or disfigurement of body parts or attributes used to attract others; and after events associated with guilt about personal activity. In addition, any event that activates strong emotions, such as erotic excitement, anger, anxiety, guilt, or shame, would be more than usually stressful, even though the person might precipitate such experiences by his behavior patterns.

Clinical studies also indicate what kinds of responses may be more frequent in the histrionic personality during and after the external stress event. Under stress, the proto-typical histrionic person becomes emotional, impulsive, unstable, and possibly disturbed in motor, perceptual, and interpretative functions.

Styles of thought, felt emotion, and subjective experi-ence are of central relevance to the present theses and have been described by Shapiro (1965). He emphasized the importance of impressionism and repression as part of this style of cognition. That is, the prototypical histrionic per-sonality lacks a sharp focus of attention and arrives quickly at a global but superficial assumption of the meaning of perceptions, memories, fantasies, and felt emotions. There is a corresponding lack of factual detail and definition in perception plus distractability and incapacity for persistent or intense concentration. The historical continuity of such perceptual and ideational styles leads to a relatively non-factual world in which guiding schemata of self, objects, and environment have a flat, depthless quality.

Dwelling conceptually in this nonfactual world pro-motes the behavioral traits of hysterical romance, emphasis on fantasy meanings, and *la belle indifference*. For example, the prototypic histrionic personality may react swiftly with an emotional outburst and yet remain unable to conceptualize what is happening and why such feelings occur. After the episode he may remember his own emotional experiences unclearly and will regard them as if visited on him rather than self-instigated.

This general style of representation of perception, thought, and emotion leads to patterns observable in interpersonal relations, traits, and communicative styles. A tabular summary of what is meant by these components of hysterical style is presented in Table 7-2.

Shapiro's formulations differ from clinical psychoanalytic opinion in terms of the stability of such patterns. Shapiro regards the patterns as relatively fixed, perhaps the result of constitutional predisposition and childhood experiences. Other analysts regard these patterns as more likely to occur during conflict. The following discussion will not contradict either position, since both allow us to assume a fixed base line of cognitive-emotional style and an intensification of such patterns during stress.

Controlling Thought and Emotion: Harry as a "Histrionic Personality"

Harry will now be considered as if he responded to stress and treatment in a typically histrionic manner. One of his six conflictual themes, as described earlier, will be used to clarify the histrionic mode of controlling thought and emotion. This theme concerns Harry's relief that he is alive when someone had to die (see A1, Table 7-1).

Considered in microgenetic form, Harry's perceptions of the dead girl's body and his own bodily sensations of

TABLE 7-2. Patterns in the Histrionic Personality Style Prototype

Information-processing style

Short-order patterns—observe in flow of thought and emotion on a topic.

- Global deployment of attention.
- Unclear or incomplete representations of ideas and feelings, possibly with lack of details or clear labels in communication, nonverbal communications not translated into words or conscious meanings.
- Only partial or unidirectional associational lines.
- Short circuit to apparent completion of problematic thoughts.

Traits

Medium-order patterns—observe in interviews.

- Attention-seeking behaviors, possibly including demands for attention, and/or the use of charm, vivacity, sex appeal, childishness.
- Fluid change in mood and emotion, possibly including breakthroughs of feeling.
- Inconsistency of apparent attitudes.

Interpersonal relations

Long-order patterns—observe in a patient's history.

- Repetitive, impulsive, stereotyped interpersonal relationships often characterized by victim–aggressor, child-parent, and rescue or rape themes.
- "Cardboard" fantasies and self-object attitudes.
- Drifting but possibly dramatic lives with an existential sense that reality is not really real.

Courtesy of Mardi J. Horowitz, *Stress Response Syndromes.*

being alive are matched with his fear of finding himself dead. The discrepancy between his perceptions and his fears leads to feelings of relief. The sense of relief is then represented as a conscious experience.

In the context of the girl's death, relief is incongruent with moral strictures. Harry believes that he should share the fate of others rather than have others absorb bad fate. This discrepancy between current and enduring concepts leads to guilt. Harry has low toleration for strong emotions, and the danger of experiencing guilt motivates efforts to repress the representations that generate the emotions.

While repression helps Harry escape unpleasant ideas and emotions, it impedes information processing. Were it not for controlling efforts, Harry might think again of the girl's death, his relief, and his attitudes toward survival at her expense. He might realize that he was following unrealistic principles of thought, forgive himself for feeling relief, undertake some act of penance and remorse if he could not change his attitude, or reach some other resolution of the incongruity between the current concept with his enduring schemata.

If repression is *what* Harry accomplishes, one can go further in microanalysis to indicate *how* it is accomplished in terms of cognitive operations. These operations can be abstracted as if they were in a hierarchy. The maneuver to try first in the hierarchy is inhibition of conscious representation. The initial perceptual images of the girl's body are too powerful to ward off and, immediately after the accident, Harry might have behaved in an "uncontrolled" hysterical style. Later, when defensive capacity is relatively stronger, the active memory images can be inhibited, counteracting the tendency toward repeated representation. Similarly, the initial ideas and feelings of relief may be too powerful to avoid, but later, as components of active memory, their reproductive tendency can be inhibited.

Suppose this inhibition fails or is only partly successful. Warded-off ideas are expressed in some modality of representation. In a secondary maneuver, the extended meanings of the ideas can still be avoided by inhibition of translation from initial modes to other forms of representation. Harry could have only his visual images and avoid verbal concepts concerning death, relief, and causation.

A third maneuver is to prevent association to meanings that have been represented. This is again, hypothetically, an interruption of an automatic response tendency. Harry might conceptualize events in image and word forms but not continue in development of obvious associational connections. The purpose would be avoidance of full conscious awareness of threatening meanings.

These controlling efforts are three typically histrionic forms of inhibition: avoidance of representation, avoidance of translation of threatening information from one mode of representation to another, and avoidance of automatic associational connections. If these efforts fail to ward off threatening concepts, there are additional methods. A fourth maneuver is the reversal of role from active to passive. Harry could avoid thinking about his own active thoughts by deploying attention to how other factors (fate, the girl, or the listener to his story) are involved. He could then change the attitude that he was alive because he *actively* wished to be alive, even if another person died, by thinking of one's *passivity* with regard to fate, of the girl's activity in hitchhiking, and of how she got herself into the accident.

The fifth and last "hysterical" maneuver is alteration of state of consciousness. Metaphorically, if the hysteric cannot prevent an idea from gaining consciousness, he removes consciousness from the idea by changing the organization of thought and the sense of self. Harry used alcohol for this purpose, but no outside agents are necessary to enter a hypnoid state, with loss of reflective self-awareness. These five cognitive maneuvers can be listed as if they were a hierarchy of "rules" for the avoidance of unwanted ideas:

1. Avoid representation.
2. Avoid intermodal translation.
3. Avoid automatic associational connections (and avoid conscious problem-solving thought).
4. Change self-attitude from active to passive (and vice versa).
5. Alter state of consciousness in order to: (1) alter hierarchies of wishes and fears; (2) blur realities and fantasies; (3) dissociate conflicting attitudes; and (4) alter the sense of self as instigator of thought and action.

The histrionic has further maneuvers, but these extend longer in time. Harry could manipulate situations so that some external person could be held responsible for his survival. This reduces the danger of a sense of guilty personal activity. In terms of very long-range maneuvers, Harry could characterologically avoid experiencing himself as ever fully real, aware, and responsible. He could identify himself with others, real or fantasied, which would make any act, or thought crime, their responsibility and not his.

Clarity in Therapeutic Interventions: an Important Nuance with Persons Who Have a Histrionic Style

If the person of histrionic style enters psychotherapy because of stress response symptoms, the therapist will try to terminate the state of stress by helping him to complete the processing of the stress-related ideas and feelings. The activity will include thinking through ideas, including latent conflicts activated by the event, experiencing emotions, and revising concepts to reduce discrepancies. The interpretation of defense may be useful to remove impediments to processing, but the main goal in the present model is to end or reduce a state of stress rather than to alter the character style. Even with such limited goals, character style must be understood and the usual therapy techniques used with appropriate nuances.

These nuances are versions, variations, or accentuations of major techniques such as clarification. One example is simple repetition of what the patient has said. The therapist may, by repeating a phrase, exert a noticeable effect on the histrionic, who may respond with a startle reaction, surprise, laughter, or other emotional expressions. The same words uttered by the therapist mean something different from when they are thought or spoken by the histrionic himself; they are to be taken more seriously.

Additional meanings accrue and some meanings are also stripped away. For example, a guilty statement by Harry, repeated by the therapist in a neutral or kind voice, may seem less heinous. More explicitly, to call this "repetition" is to be correct only in a phonemic sense. Actually, the patient hears meanings more clearly, hears new meanings as well, and the previously warded-off contents and meanings may seem less dangerous when repeated by the therapist.

Simple repetition is, of course, not so "simple." The therapist selects particular phrases and may recombine phrases to clarify by connection of causal sequences. At first, when Harry was vague about survivorship, but said "I guess I am lucky to still be around," the therapist might just say "yes" to accentuate the thought. A fuller repetition in other words, such as "you feel fortunate to have survived," may also have progressive effects; it "forces" Harry closer to the potential next thought . . . "and she did not, so I feel bad about feeling relief."

Left to his own processes, Harry might have verbalized the various "ingredients" in the theme, might even have painfully experienced pangs of guilt and anxiety, and yet might still not have really "listened" to his ideas. In response to this vague style, the therapist may pull together scattered phrases: "You had the thought, 'Gee I'm glad to still be around, but isn't it awful to be glad when she's dead?' " Harry might listen to his own ideas through the vehicle of the therapist and work out his own reassurance or acceptance. This seems preferable to giving him permission by saying, "You feel guilty over a thought that anyone would have in such a situation"; although this is, of course, sometimes necessary. As will be seen, *these simple everyday maneuvers are not as effective with persons of compulsive style.*

Other therapeutic maneuvers oriented toward helping the histrionic complete the processing of stressful events are equally commonplace. To avoid dwelling further on well-known aspects of psychotherapy, some maneuvers are listed in tabular form as applicable to specific facets of hysterical style (Table 7-3). Each maneuver listed has additional nuances. For example, with some persons with histrionic personality, interpretations or clarifications should be very short and simple, delivered in a matter-of-fact tone that would serve to counter their vagueness, emotionality, and tendency to elaborate any therapist activity into a fantasy relationship.

TABLE 7-3. Some "Defects" of the Histrionic Style
and Their Counteractants in Therapy

Function	Style as "defect"	Therapeutic counter
Perception	Global or selective inattention	Ask for details
Representation	Impressionistic rather than accurate	"Abreaction" and reconstruction
Translation of images and enactions to words	Limited	Encourage talk Provide verbal labels
Associations	Limited by inhibitions Misinterpretations based on schematic stereotypes, deflected from reality to wishes and fears	Encourage production Repetition Clarification
Problem solving	Short circuit to rapid but often erroneous conclusions Avoidance of topic when emotions are unbearable	Keep subject open Interpretations Support

Courtesy of Mardi J. Horowitz, *Stress Response Syndromes.*

Nuances of Relationship with the Histrionic Patient in a State of Stress

Histrionic persons have a low toleration for emotion, although they are touted for emotionality. Because motivations are experienced as inexorable and potentially intolerable, the ideas that evoke emotion are inhibited. If toleration for the unpleasant emotions associated with a stressful event can be increased, then cognitive processing of that event can be resumed. The therapeutic relationship protects the patient from the dangers of internal conflict and potential loss of controls, and so operates to increase tolerance for warded-off ideas and feelings. The therapist effects the patient's sense of this relationship by his or her activities or restraint. How this is typically done is also a nuance of technique.

After a stress event, the hysterical patient often manifests swings from rigid overcontrol to uncontrolled intrusions and emotional repetition. *During these swings, especially at the beginning and with a desperate patient, the therapist may oscillate between closeness and distance within the boundaries that characterize a therapeutic relationship.*

The histrionic may consider it imperative to have care and attention. This imperative need has been called, at times, the "oral," "sick," or "bad" component of some hysterical styles (Easser and Lesser 1965, Lazare 1971, Marmor 1953). During the period of imperative need, especially after a devastating stress event, the histrionic may need to experience warmth and human support from the therapist. Without it, the therapeutic relationship will fall apart, the patient may regress or develop further psychopathology. During this phase the therapist moves, in effect, closer to the patient: just close enough to provide necessary support and not so "close" as the patient *appears* to wish.

As the patient becomes more comfortable, he may begin to feel anxiety at the degree of intimacy in the therapeutic relationship because there may be a fear of being seduced or enthralled by the therapist. The therapist then moves back to a "cooler" or more "distant" stance.

The therapist thus oscillates to keep the patient within a zone of safety by sensitive modification of his manner of relating to the patient. Safety allows the patient to move in the direction of greater conceptual clarity (Sandler 1960, Weiss 1971). Naturally, the therapist's manner includes his nonverbal and verbal cues. This is what the therapist *allows* himself to do in the context of his own real responses and qualities of being. This is *not* role playing. The therapist allows or inhibits his own response tendencies as elicited by the patient.

If the therapist does not oscillate in from a relatively *distant* position, and if the patient has urgent needs for stabilizing his self-concept through relational support, then the discrepancy between need and supply will be so painful that the patient will find it unendurable to expose problematic lines of thought. Inhibition would continue. If the therapist does not oscillate from a relatively *close* position, then conceptual processing will begin but transference issues will cloud working through the stress response syndrome. Neither clarity nor oscillation by the therapist may be a suitable nuance of technique with the obsessional.

COMPULSIVE STYLE IN RESPONSE TO STRESS

Background

Contemporary theory of compulsive style evolved from analysis of neurotic obsessions, compulsions, doubts, and irrational fears. Abraham (1924) and Freud (1909) believed the obsessional neuroses to be secondary to regressions to or fixations at the anal-sadistic phase of psychosexual development. The manifestations of the neuroses were seen as compromises between aggressive and sexual impulsive aims and defenses such as isolation, intellectualization, reaction formation, and undoing. Underneath a rational consciousness, ambivalent and magical thinking were noted to be prominent. Common conflicts were formed in the interaction of aggressive impulses and predispositions to rage, fears of assault, and harsh attitudes of morality and duty. These conflicts lead to coexistence and fluctuation of dominance and submission themes in interpersonal situations and fantasies.

Salzman (1968) emphasized the compulsive sense of being driven, his strivings for omniscience and control, and his concerns for the magical effects of unfriendly thoughts of both the self and others. Homosexual thoughts may also intrude, although often without homosexual behavior.

Since compulsives tend more toward acute awareness of ideas, staying with one position threatens to lead to unpleasant emotions. Seeing the self as dominant is associated with sadism to others and leads to guilt. Seeing the self as submissive is associated with weakness and fears of assaults; hence, this position evokes anxiety. Alternation between opposing poles, as in alternation between sadistic-dominance themes and passive-submissive themes, serves to undo the danger of remaining at either pole (Sampson et al. 1972, Weiss, 1967).

To avoid stabilization at a single position and to accomplish the defense of undoing, compulsives often use the cognitive operation of shifting from one aspect of a theme to an opposi-

tional aspect and back again. The result is continuous change. At the expense of decision and decisiveness, the obsessional maintains a sense of control and avoids emotional threats (Barnett 1972, Schwartz 1972, Silverman 1972).

While the compulsive moves so rapidly that emotions do not gain full awareness, he or she cannot totally eliminate feelings. Some compulsives have intrusions of feelings either in minor quasi-ideational form, or as expressed in attacks of rage. Even when this occurs, however, the event can be undone by what Salzman calls "verbal juggling." This process includes alterations of meaning, the use of formulas to arrive at attitudes or plans, shifts in valuation from over- to underestimation, and, sometimes, the attribution of magical properties to word labels.

Shapiro (1965) has described the narrowed focus of the mode of attention of the compulsive person, how it misses certain aspects of the world while it engages others in detail. Ideal flexibility of attention involves smooth shifts between sharply directed attention and more impressionistic forms of cognition. The compulsive lacks such fluidity.

He also describes how the compulsive is driven in the course of his thought, emotion, and behavior by "shoulds" and "oughts" dictated by a sense of duty, by his fears of loss of control, and by his need to inhibit recognition of his "wants." In spite of his usual capacity for hard work, productivity, and "will power," the compulsive person may experience difficulty and discomfort when a decision is to be made. Instead of deciding on the basis of wishes and fears, the compulsive must maintain a sense of omnipotence and, therefore, must avoid the dangerous mistakes inherent in a trial-and-error world. The decision among possible choices is likely to rest on a rule evoked to guarantee a "right" decision or else is made on impulse, to end the anxiety. The result of these cognitive styles is an experiential distance from felt emotion. The exception is a feeling of anxious self-doubt, a mood instigated by the absence of cognitive closure.

This discussion has focused on aspects of cognitive style. These are summarized in Table 7-4 with common traits and patterns of behavior. I will be using the terms compulsive and obsessional interchangeably for this style.

Controlling Thought and Emotion: Harry as Having a Compulsive Style

Stressful events may so compel interest that there may be little difference in the initial registration and experience of persons with histrionic or compulsive style. But, short of extreme disasters, the obsessional person may remain behaviorally calm and emotionless in contrast to the emotional explosions of the histrionic personality. (This report demands such generalizations, but it should be noted that during some events, obsessionals may become quite emotional and histrionics may remain calm. The difference remains in the quality of the person's conscious experience. The histrionic person can have a "hysterical calm" because it is based on an inhibition of some aspects of potential knowledge; no emotion occurs because implications are not known. If and when the obsessional behaves emotionally, it may be experienced by him as a loss of control, one to be "undone" by retrospective shifts of meaning, rituals, apologies, or self-recriminations.)

TABLE 7-4. Patterns in the Compulsive Personality Style Prototype

Information-processing style

Short-order patterns—observe in flow of thought and emotion on a topic.

- Sharp focus attention on details.
- Clear representation of ideas, meager representation of emotions.
- Shifting organization and implications of ideas rather than following an associational line to conclusion as directed by original intent or intrinsic meanings.
- Avoiding completion on decision or a given problem, instead switching back and forth between attitudes.

Traits

Medium-order patterns—observe in interviews.

- Doubt, worry, overly detailed productivity and/or procrastination.
- Single-minded, unperturbable, intellectualizing.
- Tense, deliberate, unenthusiastic.
- Rigid, ritualistic.

Interpersonal relations

Long-order patterns—observe in a patient's history.

- Develops regimented, routine, and continuous interpersonal relationships low in "life," vividness, or pleasure. Often frustrating to be with.
- Prone to dominance-submission themes or power and control struggles
- Duty filling, hardworking, seeks or makes strain and pressure, does what one should do rather than what one decides to do.
- Experiences self as remote from emotional connection with others, although feels committed to operating with others because of role or principles.

Courtesy of Mardi J. Horowitz, *Stress Response Syndromes.*

After a stressful event, both types may exhibit similar general stress response tendencies, including phases of denial and intrusion. But they may differ in their stability in any given phase. The compulsive type may be able to maintain the period of emotional numbing with greater stability; the histrionic type may be able to tolerate phases of episodic intrusions with more apparent stability and less narcissistic injury.

During the oscillatory phase, when the uncompleted images and ideas of the current stressful concepts tend to repeated and intrusive representation, the person of a histrionic prototype is likely to inhibit representation to ward off these unwelcome mental contents. The obsessional may be precise and clear in describing the intrusive images, but may focus on details related to "duty," for example, and away from the simple emotion-evoking meanings of the gestalt of the image.

It is during the oscillatory phase of both intrusions and warding-off maneuvers that styles stand out in starkest form. Instead of, or in addition to, repressive maneuvers as listed earlier, the compulsive responds to threatened repetitions with cognitive maneuvers such as shifting. By a shift to "something else," the obsessional is able to jam cognitive channels and prevent emergence of warded-off contents, or to so shift meanings as to stifle emotional arousal. That is, by shifting from topic to topic, or from one meaning to another meaning of the same topic, the emotion-arousing properties of one set of implications are averted.

Treating Harry

In discussion of a histrionic Harry, the theme of survival guilt was used as an example. A compulsive Harry might share a tendency toward emergence of the same theme but react to this threat with a style characterized by shifting rather than vagueness and inhibition.

In psychotherapy, Harry begins to talk of the unbidden images of the girl's body. He associates now to his memory of feeling relieved to be alive. The next conceptualization, following the idealized line of working through, outlined earlier, *would be* association of his relieved feelings with ideas of survival at her expense. This cluster *would be* matched against moral strictures counter to such personal gain through damage to others, and Harry *would* go on to conceptualize his emotional experience of guilt or shame (theme A1 in Table 7-1). Once clear, he could revise his schematic belief that someone had to die, accept his relief, feel remorse, even plan a penance, and reduce incongruity through one or more of these changes.

Harry does not follow this idealized route because the potential of these emotional experiences is appraised as intolerable at a not fully conscious level of information processing. A switch is made to another ideational cycle in order to avoid the first one. The second cycle is also associatively related to the images of the girl's body. A common element in both ideational cycles allows a pivotal change and reduces awareness that the subtopic has changed (Klein 1967).

The pivot for the switch is the idea of bodily damage. In the second ideational cluster, the concept is that bodily damage could happen to him, perhaps at any future time, since it has now happened to her. Through the comparison with his wishes for invulnerability and his dread of vulnerability, fear is aroused (B1 in Table 7-1).

While fear is unpleasant and threatening as a potential

experience, the switch allows movement away from the potential feelings of guilt (theme A1). When the second theme (B1) becomes too clear, fear might be consciously experienced. The procedure can be reversed with return to A1. Harry can oscillate in terms of conscious and communicative meanings between A1 and B1 without either set of dangerous ideas and emotions being fully experienced.

Harry need not limit switching operations to the two contexts for ideas about bodily damage. He can switch between any permutation of any theme. He can transform, reverse, or undo guilt with fear or anger (Jones 1929). He can see himself as victim, then aggressor, then victim, and so forth. These shifts dampen emotional responsivity but reduce cognitive processing of themes.

This does not imply that inhibition of representation will not be found in compulsive Harry or that shifts of theme will be absent in histrionic Harry. Obsessional Harry will attempt inhibitions and use his shifts when inhibitory efforts fail. Hysterical Harry might shift from active to passive, as noted earlier, but timing and quality of the shifts would differ. Obsessional Harry would tend to shift more rapidly, with less vagueness at either pole. The shift could occur in midphrase, between an utterance of his and a response from the therapist, or even as virtually simultaneous trains of thought.

It is because of rapid shifts that therapists who attempt clarity with obsessionals may be thwarted in their task. Suppose the therapist makes a clarifying intervention about A1, the survivor guilt theme. Compulsive Harry may have already shifted to B1, his fear of body injury, and thus hear the remarks in a noncongruent state. The clarification procedure may not work well because Harry was not unclear or vague in the first place, is not listening from the earlier position, and will undo the therapist's intervention by further shifts. An interpretation to the effect that Harry fears bodily damage as a retribution for his survivor relief and guilt would be premature since, at this point, he has not fully experienced either the fear or the guilt.

Holding to Context: Important Nuances with Persons Who Have a Compulsive Style

Holding the obsessional to a topic or to a given context within a topic is equivalent to clarifying for the histrionic type. *Metaphorically, the compulsive avoids conceptual time where the hysteric avoids conceptual space. The goal of holding is reduction of shifting, so that the patient can progress further along a given conceptual process.* The patient must also be helped to tolerate the emotions that will be experienced when he cannot quickly divert ideas into and out of conscious awareness.

Holding to context is more complicated than clarification. One begins with at least two current problems, such as the dual themes of A1 and B1 in Harry. When the patient is not shifting with extreme rapidity, the therapist may simply hold the patient to either one or the other theme.

The patient will not comply with this maneuver and the therapist must not confuse "holding" with "forcing." Ferenczi (1950), in an effort to speed up analysis, experimented with various ways to make the obsessional stay on topic until intensely felt emotions occurred. For example, he insisted that his patient develop and maintain visual fantasies relevant to a specific theme. During this technical maneuver his obsessional patients did experience emotions; they even had affective explosions, but the transference complications impeded rather than enhanced the therapy.

The therapist has to shift, even though he attempts to hold the patient to a topic. That is, the therapist shifts at a slower rate than the patient, like a dragging anchor that slows the process. This operation increases the progress of the patient in both directions. That is, with each shift, he is able to go a bit further along the conceptual route of either theme, even though he soon becomes frightened and crowds the theme out of mind with an alternative.

The therapist may use repetitions, as with the hysteric, in order to hold or slow the shift of an obsessional patient. But this use of the same maneuver is done with a different nuance. With the hysteric, the repetition heightens the meaning of what the patient is *now* saying. With the obsessional, the repetition goes back to what the patient was saying *before* the shift away from the context occurred. With the histrionic, the repetition may be short phrases. With the obsessional, greater length may be necessary, in order to state the specific context that is being warded off. For example, if Harry is talking about bodily damage and shifts from a survivor guilt context to his fears of injury, then a repetition by the therapist has to link bodily damage specifically to the survivor guilt theme. With the hysteric, such wordy interventions might only diminish clarity.

At times, this more extensive repetition in the compulsive may include the technique of going back to the very beginning of an exchange, retracing the flow carefully, and indicating where extraneous or only vaguely relevant details were introduced by the patient. Reconstructions may add warded-off details. This technique has been suggested for long-term character analysis (Salzman 1968, Weiss 1971), during which defensive operations are interpreted so that the patient increases conscious control and diminishes unconscious restrictions on ideas and feelings. In shorter therapy, aimed at working through a stress, this extensive repetition is still useful, because, during the review by the therapist, the patient attends to the uncomfortable aspects of the topic.

Increased time on the topic allows more opportunity for processing and hence moves the patient toward completion. Emotions aroused by the flow of ideas are more tolerable within the therapeutic relationship than for the patient alone. Also, time on the topic and with the therapist allows continued processing in a communicative state, emphasizing reality and problem solving rather than fantasy and magical belief systems. Identification with and externalization onto the relatively neutral therapist also allows temporary reduction in rigid and harsh introjects that might otherwise deflect thought.

Focusing on details is sometimes a partial deterrent to shifting in the compulsive, just as it may aid clarity with the histrionic type. The nuances of focusing on details differ because the purposes differ. In general, the aim with the hysteric is to move from concrete, experiential information, such as images, toward more abstract or more extended meanings, such as word labels for activities and things. The aim with the obsessional is to move from abstract levels, where shifts are facile, to a concrete context. Details act as pegs of meaning in concrete contexts, and make shifts of attitude more difficult. This maneuver utilizes the obsessional's predisposition to details but allows the therapist to specifically select them. Again, the nuance of asking for concrete details is part of the general aim of increasing conceptualization time.

In states where shifts are so rapid as to preclude simple repetition or questioning, the therapist may use a more complex form of repetition. The therapist repeats the event, for example, Harry's intrusive image of the girl's body, and then repeats in a single package the disparate attitudes that the patient oscillates between. For example, the therapist might tell Harry that the image of the girl's body led to two themes. One was the idea of relief at being spared from death that made him feel frightened and guilty. The other was the idea of bodily harm to himself. Were the rate of oscillation less rapid, this form of "packaged" intervention would not be as necessary, since simpler holding operations may be sufficient and the therapist can focus on a single theme.

These efforts by the therapist encroach on the habitual style of the patient. The patient may respond by minimizing or exaggerating the meaning of the intervention. The obsessional is especially vulnerable to threats to his sense of omniscience, especially after traumatic events. If the therapist holds him on a topic, the obsessional senses warded-off ideas and feelings and develops uncertainties that cause his self-esteem to fall.

To protect the patient's self-esteem, the therapist uses another technical nuance. He uses questioning to accomplish clarification and topic deepening, even when he has an interpretation in mind. The questions aim the patient toward answers that contain the important, warded-off, but now emerging ideas. The obsessional patient can then credit himself with expressing these ideas and experiencing these feelings. The therapist with the hysterical person might, in contrast, interpret at such a moment, using a firm, short delivery, since a question might be followed by vagueness.

To the obsessional, incisive interpretations often mean that the therapist knows something he does not know. A transference bind over dominance and submission arises as the patient either rebels against the interpretation with stubborn denial, accepts it meekly without thinking about it, or both.

Timing is also important with compulsives working through stress-activated themes. After experience with a given patient, the therapist intuitively knows when a shift is about to take place. At just that moment, or a trifle before, the therapist asks his question. This interrupts the shift and increases conceptual "time and space" on the topic about to be warded off. These technical nuances are put in a crude, broad context in Table 7-5.

Nuances of Relationship with Compulsive Patients in a State of Stress

The oscillation described as sometimes necessary with the histrionic style is not as advisable with the obsessional style. Instead, the therapist creates a safe situation for the patient by remaining stable within his own clear boundaries (e.g., objectivity, compassion, understanding, concern for the truth, or whatever his own personal and professional traits are).

TABLE 7-5. Some Defects of Compulsive Style
and Their Counteractants in Therapy

Function	Style as "defect"	Therapeutic counter
Perception	Detailed and factual	Ask for overall impressions and statements about emotional experiences
Representation	Isolation of ideas from emotions	Link emotional meanings to ideational meanings
Translation of images to words	Misses emotional meaning in a rapid transition to partial word meanings	Focus attention on images and felt reactions to them
Associations	Shifts sets of meanings back and forth	Holding operations Interpretation of defense and of warded off meanings
Problem solving	Endless rumination without reaching decisions	Interpretation of reasons for warding off clear decisions

Courtesy of Mardi J. Horowitz, *Stress Response Syndromes.*

The patient learns the limits of the therapist within this frame. It gives him faith that the therapist will react neither harshly nor seductively. This trust increases *the patient's* breadth of oscillation. He can express more aggressive ideas, if he knows the therapist will neither submit, be injured, compete for dominance, or accuse him of evil.

Harry could express more of his bodily worries when he knew the therapist would not himself feel guilty or overresponsible.

If the therapist changes with the compulsive's tests or needs, then the obsessional worries that he may be too powerful, too weak, or too "sick" for the therapist to handle. Also, the obsessional may use the situation to externalize warded-off ideas or even defensive maneuvers. The therapist shifts, not he. This is not to say the obsessional does not, at times, need kindly support after disastrous external events. But his propensity for shifting makes changes in the degree of support more hazardous than a consistent attitude, whether kindly supportive, neutral-tough, or otherwise.

Suppose the therapist becomes more kindly as Harry goes through a turbulent period of emotional expression of guilt over survival. Harry may experience this as an increase in the therapist's concern or worry for him. He might shift from the "little" suffering position that elicited the therapist's reaction, to a "big" position from which he looks down with contempt at the "worried" therapist.

Similarly, if the therapist is not consistently tough-minded, in the ordinary sense of insisting on information and truth-telling, but shifts to this stance only in response to the patient's stubborn evasiveness, then the patient can shift from strong stubbornness to weak, vulnerable self-concepts. Within the context of this shift, the therapist comes to be experienced as hostile, demeaning, and demanding.

Unlike the hysteric, then *the obsessional's shifts in role and attitude within the therapeutic situation are likely to be out of phase with changes in demeanor of the therapist.* The obsessional can chance further and more lucid swings in state when he senses the stability of the therapist.

Transference resistances will occur in spite of the therapist's effort to maintain a therapeutic relationship. The stability of the therapist will be exaggerated by the patient into an omniscience that he will continually test. When negative transference reactions occur, the therapist will act to resolve those that interfere with the goals of therapy. But some transference reactions will not be negative even though they act as resistances. The hysteric may demand attention and halt progress to get it. The obsessional may take an oppositional stance not so much out of hostility or stubbornness, although such factors will be present, as out of a need to avoid the dangerous intimacy of agreement and cooperation. Since the therapist is not aiming at analysis of transference to effect character change, he need not interpret this process. Instead, with change, he need not interpret this process. Instead, with an obsessional patient in an oppositional stance, he may word his interventions to take advantage of the situation.

That is, interventions can be worded, when necessary, in an oppositional manner. Suppose Harry was talking about picking up the girl and the therapist knew he was predisposed to feeling guilty but was warding it off. With a hysterical Harry the therapist might say, "You feel bad about picking up the girl." With an obsessional and cooperative Harry he might say, "Could you be blaming yourself for picking up the girl?" With an oppositional obsessional stance, the therapist might say, "So you don't feel at all bad about picking up the girl." This kind of Harry may disagree and talk of his guilt feelings.

Provided the context is a basically stable therapeutic

relationship, one in which the patient has an image of the therapist as objective, kindly, and firmly competent, the inflection need not be the sincere, neutral, firm tone helpful with hysterics. *Slight* sarcasm or *mild* humor may help the obsessional Harry assume a tough position while trying out his own tender ideas (Salzman 1968).

By sternness, as implied in the above comments, the therapist may have the effect of "ordering" the obsessional to contemplate warded-off ideas. This seeming unkindness is kind in that it removes responsibility from the patient and permits him to think the unthinkable. But this sternness, mild sarcasm, or slight humor has to remain a relatively consistent characteristic of the therapist.

This is not as difficult as it may sound, for *these nuances involve what the therapist allows himself to do or not do in natural response to the situation. They are not assumed or artificial roles or traits.* For some therapists, kindliness, openness, gentleness, and a nonjudgmental air are preferable nuances to any toughness, sternness, sarcasm, or humor and may accomplish the same purpose. These latter remarks are meant more as illustrations than assertions because it is here that we encounter that blurred border between the "science" and "art" of psychotherapy.

CONCLUSION

This report has taken a state of stress, considered the variations between two dispositional types within that state, and discussed the nuances of psychodynamic psychotherapy aimed at symptom relief. These dimensions, state, typology, and mode of treatment define a frame of reference. Assertions have been made that are clearly positioned within this frame of reference. For example, stress response syndromes have been characterized by phases of denial and intrusion; hysterical persons have been described as using inhibition of representation to ward off intrusive and repetitive ideas and feelings, and clarity has been posited as an important nuance of their therapy. Obsessional persons were characterized by switching operations for the same purpose, and holding operations were asserted to be important nuances of technique in their therapy.

Such assertions involve standard psychiatric knowledge. What is gained through this model is an organization for the systematic assemblage of such knowledge. With clear conceptual positionings of assertions, many of the arguments and divergencies that characterize psychiatry and psychology would fall away in favor of renewed empirical observation and formulation. The key is comparable rather than incongruous levels of abstraction.

To the extent that the model is worthwhile, the assertions here can be specifically challenged. General stress response tendencies may not follow the pathways defined; there may be better ways to typologize what was called "hysterical" and "obsessional"; the nuances of focused psychodynamic psychotherapy described may be incomplete or inappropriate. A specific site of disagreement can be localized by following the same dimensions. For example, *an argument about a nuance of treatment would have to be connected with a specific kind of person, in an intrusive-repetitive phase after a stressful external event, involved in psychodynamic treatment aimed at relief of intrusions and resolution of the state of stress.*

While this type of model localizes conceptualization, it

may be argued that it defines restrictively small areas. Within the general field of psychopathology and psychotherapy there would be multitudes of such areas. I believe that the field is so large that many specific subdivisions are indicated, and that knowledge will be accumulated and clarified by this method. The complexity is not overwhelming. The present model can be extended by keeping any two dimensions constant while extending the boundaries of the third. For example, extensions may involve other variations of personality, other versions of pathological states, and other views of therapy.

Variations in typology would include narcissistic, schizoid, impulsive, and paranoid personalities. Each would be contrasted with hysterical and obsessional styles of response to stressful life events. Each would be considered in the context of brief dynamic therapy aimed at working through the life event, and so central conceptual anchoring would be maintained.

Variations in state would include other formulations of the meaning of a crisis episode. For example, a contrasting view within the framework of brief psychodynamic therapy regards the life events as secondary in importance to enduring conflicts. The predominant state is seen as character patterns rather than phases of stress response. Separation from a lover would be seen as an occasion to work further on dependency-independency conflicts present for a long time (Mann 1973, Sifneos 1973). Would the same nuances of treatment for varying styles apply in therapy oriented toward character conflicts?

Variations in treatment would maintain the set of stress response syndromes in certain common character types. Other technical approaches would provide contrasting points of view. For example, a behavior therapist would discuss treatment of such intrusive images as noted in Harry. He might advocate such approaches as systematic desensitization and implosion (Yates 1970). Learning theory hypotheses would be advanced equivalent to the repetition-until-completion tendency described in this paper. A rationale of treatment would be based on these hypotheses. Assertions would be advanced about how systematic desensitization and implosion work. The behavior therapist might assert that desensitization would be more suitable for hysterical styles because there is a progressive clarification of anxiety-provoking representations and a supportive patient-therapist relationship. He might prefer implosive techniques for obsessional styles, as this method can hold attention to a specific aspect of an ideational complex, provoke emotional response, and engage the patient in a "tough" appearing role-relationship.

These nuances of techniques within a behavior therapy point of view could then be contrasted with the assertions of the dynamic point of view, as well as with other technical possibilities. Nuances across schools might be developed. Histrionic vagueness might be seen as altered by any clarification technique such as role playing, psychodrama, transactional analysis, or gestalt therapy. Obsessional shifting of topics might be seen as altered by any holding technique such as systematic desensitization, implosion, or guided imagery techniques. Contrary assertions would, at least, be assembled at similar levels of abstraction. Disagreements could be resolved by further observation of given types of persons in a given state. In this way we might hope to pass beyond brand names as our professional disagreements become productive rather than schismatic.

REFERENCES

Abraham, K. (1924). A short study of the development of the libido, viewed in the light of mental disorders. In *Selected Papers of Karl Abraham*, ed. E. Jones, pp. 418–501. London: Hogarth, 1948.

Appelgarth, A. (1971). Comments on aspects of the theory of psychic energy. *Journal of the American Psychoanalytic Association* 19:379–416.

Barnett, J. (1972). Therapeutic intervention in the dysfunctional thought processes of the obsessional. *American Journal of Psychotherapy* 26:338–351.

Bibring, E. (1954). Psychoanalysis and the dynamic psychotherapies. *Journal of the American Psychoanalytic Association* 2:745–770.

Bowlby, J., and Parkes, C. M. (1970). Separation and loss within the family. In *The International Yearbook for Child Psychiatry and Allied Disciplines*, ed. E. J. Anthony and C. Kopernik, pp. 197–215. New York: Wiley.

Davis, D. R. (1966). *An Introduction to Psychopathology*. London: Oxford University Press.

Easser, B. R., and Lesser, S. R. (1965). Hysterical personality: a re-evaluation. *Psychoanalytic Quarterly* 34:390–405.

Ferenczi, S. (1950). *Further Contributions to the Theory and Technique of Psychoanalysis*. London: Hogarth and the Institute of Psychoanalysis.

French, T. (1952). *The Integration of Behavior. Vol. 1: Basic Postulates*. Chicago: University of Chicago Press.

Freud, S. (1893). On the psychical mechanism of hysterical phenomena. *Standard Edition* 3:25–39.

——— (1909). Notes upon a case of obsessional neurosis. In *Collected Papers* 3:165. London: Hogarth, 1949.

——— (1920). Beyond the pleasure principle. *Standard Edition* 18:7–64.

_____ (1926). Inhibitions, symptoms and anxiety. *Standard Edition* 20:87–172.

Freud, S., and Breuer, J. (1893–1895). Studies on hysteria. *Standard Edition* 2:185–305.

Furst, S. S. (1967). Psychic trauma: a survey. In *Psychic Trauma*, ed. S. S. Furst, pp. 3–50. New York: Basic Books.

Greenson, R. (1965). The working alliance and the transference neurosis. *Psychoanalytic Quarterly* 34:155–181.

Grinker, K., and Spiegel, S. (1945). *Men Under Stress*. Philadelphia: Blakiston.

Hamburg, D. A., and Adams, J. E. (1967). A perspective on coping behavior: seeking and utilizing information in major transitions. *Archives of General Psychiatry* 17:277–284.

Horowitz, M. J. (1973). Phase oriented treatment of stress response syndromes. *American Journal of Psychotherapy* 27:506–515.

_____ (1986). *Stress Response Syndrome*. 2nd ed. Northvale, NJ: Jason Aronson.

Horowitz, M. J., and Becker, S. S. (1972). Cognitive response to stress: experimental studies of a compulsion to repeat trauma. In *Psychoanalysis and Contemporary Science*, vol. 1, ed. R. Holt and E. Peterfreund, pp. 258–305. New York: Macmillan.

Janet, P. (1965). *The Major Symptoms of Hysteria*. New York: Hafner.

Janis, I. L. (1969). *Stress and Frustration*. New York: Harcourt-Brace-Jovanovich.

Jones, E. (1929). Fear, guilt and hate. *International Journal of Psycho-Analysis* 10:383–397.

Klein, G. S. (1967). Peremptory ideation: structure and force in motivated ideas. *Psychological Issues* 5:80–128.

Lazare, A. (1971). The hysterical character in psychoanalytic theory: evolution and confusion. *Archives of General Psychiatry* 25:131–137.

Lazarus, R. S. (1966). *Psychological Stress and the Coping Process.* New York: McGraw-Hill.

Lazarus, R. S., and Folkman, S. K. (1984). *Stress, Appraisal and Coping.* New York: Springer.

Lifton, R. J. (1967). *History and Human Survival.* New York: Vantage Books.

Ludwig, A. M. (1972). Hysteria: a neurobiological theory. *Archives of General Psychiatry* 27:771–777.

Mann, J. (1973). *Time Limited Psychotherapy.* Cambridge, MA: Harvard University Press.

Marmor, J. (1953). Orality in the hysterical personality. *Journal of the American Psychoanalytic Association* 1:656–675.

Miller, G. A., Galanter, E., and Pribram, K. (1960). *Plans and the Structure of Behavior.* New York: Henry Holt.

Peterfreund, E. (1971). Information systems and psychoanalysis: an evolutionary, biological approach to psychoanalytic theory. *Psychological Issues* 7:1–397.

Pribram, K. H. (1967). Emotion: steps toward a neuropsychological theory. In *Neurophysiology and Emotion,* ed. D. Glass, pp. 3–40. New York: Rockefeller University Press and Russell Sage.

Salzman, L. (1968). *The Obsessive Personality.* New York: Science House.

Sampson, H., Weiss, J., and Mlodnosky, L. (1972). Defense analysis and the emergence of warded-off mental contents: an empirical study. *Archives of General Psychiatry* 26:524–532.

Sandler, J. (1960). The background of safety. *International Journal of Psycho-Analysis* 41:352–356.

Schwartz, E. K. (1972). The treatment of the obsessive patient in the group therapy setting. *American Journal of Psychotherapy* 26: 352–361.

Shapiro, D. (1965). *Neurotic Styles.* New York: Basic Books.

Sifneos, P. E. (1973). *Short-Term Psychotherapy and Emotional Crisis.* Cambridge, MA: Harvard University Press.

Silverman, J. S. (1972). Obsessional disorders in childhood and adolescence. *American Journal of Psychotherapy* 26: 362–377.

Weiss, J. (1967). The integration of defenses. *International Journal of Psycho-Analysis* 48:520–524.

——— (1971). The emergence of new themes: a contribution to the psychoanalytic theory of therapy. *International Journal of Psycho-Analysis* 52:459–467.

Yates, A. O. (1970). *Behavior Therapy*. New York: Wiley.

8

Sliding Meanings in Narcissistic Personalities

Narcissism has been regarded as an important aspect of human character throughout recorded history. It is summarized in Ecclesiastes, "Vanity of vanities; all is vanity." Freud's (1914) explorations of the unconscious led him to emphasize the compensatory nature of such vanity, and Adler (1916) centered a psychology on inferiority and narcissistic compensations for deflated self-concepts. Recently, there has been a major resurgence of interest in the psychodynamics of the narcissistic character (Kernberg 1970, 1974, Kohut 1966, 1968, 1971, 1972). Pertinent to such interest is the question of how persons of a narcissistic character respond to the inevitable stresses of life, such as injury or loss.

General stress-response syndromes are known to be characterized by a tendency to compulsive repetition of ideas and feelings about the stress event (Freud 1920, Furst 1967, Horowitz 1973). Intrusive repetitions, for example, are observed in persons of varied character style. But each person may use a fairly idiosyncratic defense to ward off this general tendency to painful ideas and feelings after stressful life events. Persons with hysterical personality styles may cloud meaning while obsessionals may avoid the pangs of recurrent, stress-related emotion by undoing. In this chapter, the typical narcissistic response of sliding meanings is discussed, as well as the nuances of therapy that help alter this defensive avoidance.

BACKGROUND

Freud (1914) used the concept of narcissism as a polarity between self-centeredness and relationships with others. He characterized some syndromes as "narcissistic neuroses," a now defunct term meaning syndromes characterized by a withdrawal of interest in others. The contrasting set of syndromes, "transference neuroses," were those in which interest, however distorted, remained centered on other persons. This duality was based on a theoretical position that psychic energy, in the form of libido, was distributed either toward self or toward objects, and that libido was in limited supply, so that increased self-concern would mean decreased concern with others.

This theory has since been rejected because it does not conform well enough with clinical observations. Instead, the development of self-interest and self-concepts is now seen in two simultaneous, interrelated, but partially independent series. In one series the self-representation and self-regard are gradually evolved as independent functions. In the other series there is interdependence of one person and another, that is, self-representation and self-regard are gradually evolved in relationship to the development of object representations, object interests, and patterns of self-and-object transaction (Kohut 1971). Increased narcissism can be motivated by either a need to compensate for a deflated self-concept, without associated withdrawal of interest from objects, or by a problem in relationships with others that must be handled by increased self-interest (Kernberg 1966).

In the narcissistic character, an exquisite vulnerability of the self-concept is hypothesized to underlie a more superficial self-love, grandiosity, or idealization of others regarded as appendages to the self (self-objects). In psychoanalytic reconstructions, vulnerability of the self, the tendency to fragmented self-images under stress, has been traced to difficulties during the period of differentiating the self from the mother or other early parenting figure (Mahler 1968). Dominance of narcissistic traits in either or both parents may predispose a child to difficulties in developing a stable and independent self-representation because the parents may treat the child as if he were a function of themselves rather than a separate entity.

Being an only child or having a real or "special endowment" projected by a parent may build into the child a sense of unusual importance that is doomed to a rude awakening when he moves socially beyond the central family. That is, any atmosphere that encourages and gratifies inflated self-representations will also predispose a child to traumas when realistic limitations, inability to perform, or depreciating types of interpersonal treatment are encountered. Such encounters will also occur in the family when the child develops enough will and ability to contest parental superiority and power, and to feel betrayed and let down when his own power is insufficient to gain his own goals.

NARCISSISTIC RESPONSE TO STRESS

When the habitual narcissistic gratifications that come from being adored, given special treatment, and admiring the self are destroyed, the results may be depression, hypochondriasis, anxiety, shame, self-destructiveness, or rage directed toward any other person who can be blamed for the troubled situation. The child can learn to avoid these painful emotional states by acquiring a narcissistic mode of information processing. Such learning may be innovative, by trial and error, or it may be internalized by identification with parental modes of dealing with stressful information. The central pillar of this narcissistic style is externalization of bad attributes and internalization of good attributes in order to stabilize the self-concept. These operations demand distortion of reality and imply either a willingness to corrupt fidelity and reality, a low capacity to appraise and reappraise reality and fantasy, or a high capacity to disguise the distortions. The disguises are accomplished by shifting meanings and exaggerating and minimizing bits of reality as a nidus for fantasy elaboration.

Distortions in self-concept achieved by selective externalizations often lead to various clusters of self-related information. That is, the narcissistic mode of information processing predisposes the child to several sets of self-representations as well as incompletely developed and unrealistic sets of object-representations.

Three coexistent but split apart self-concepts that are common in narcissistic personalities have been described by Kohut (1971). They are (1) the grandiose self in which there is an inflated, exaggerated, exhibitionistic self-image, (2) the poorly esteemed, shamed, and vulnerable self-image, and (3) the dangerously chaotic, shattered, fragmented self-image. Complementary images for parent figures are maintained and include the idealized figure which, by caring or attending, will bolster low self-esteem and inflate it by reflections of "glory," as well as the mirroring figure, which will support the grandiose self-image by serving as admirer, source of praise, and evidence of personal power.

These prototypical self- and object-representations are heavily balanced toward self-concern, and interpersonal relations will be more characterized by "I-it" than "I-Thou" relationships as described by Buber (1878). As is also common in obsessional personalities, issues of power and control will be prominent in interpersonal relations, but with important differences. The obsessional is involved in an intrapsychic and perhaps interpersonal struggle over the distribution of power between himself and a significant other. The goal is gratification of certain interpersonal desires or avoidance of certain interpersonal threats. The narcissistic personality is concerned with possessing the power to enhance his or her *own* sense of competence and control, or with self-enhancement through affiliation with a powerful person. Similarly, the obsessional and the hysteric may wish to be admired by another person as part of a core wish for closeness, even homosexual closeness. The narcissistic personality also desires admiration from the other person, but the core of this desire is the use of admiration or closeness to maintain self-esteem.

The narcissistic personality is especially vulnerable to personal deflations or loss of those who support his self-concept. When he is faced with such stress events as criticism, loss of self-objects, withdrawal of praise, or humiliation, he may deny, disavow, negate, or shift in meaning the information involved to prevent a reactive state of rage, depression, or shame. If such measures should fail, there may be, in addition to externalization of bad attributes and internalization of good qualities, a shift not only in affect but in global "being." This change in state includes changes in self-imagery, demeanor, and style. If the stress event, for example, a personal criticism, leads to a mild level of threat, then the behavioral response may be an increased effort toward obtaining external "narcissistic supplies." That is, there may be a search for persons to erase criticism or supply praise, or persons whose idealized power is viewed as a useful umbrella that can be extended over the self. Much like the histrionic personality, the narcissistic makes efforts to woo or win attention from sources which enhance self-esteem.

If the stress event is of greater magnitude, or if restorative efforts as outlined above should fail, then more extreme narcissistic deviations from realistic information-processing occur. The goal of these deflections from knowing reality is to prevent a potentially catastrophic state in which a cohesive sense of self is lost. The hazard is not simply guilt because ideals have not been met. The loss of a good and coherent self-feeling, if it occurs, is associated with intensely experienced emotions such as shame and depression, plus an anguished sense of helplessness and disorientation. *To prevent this state, the narcissistic personality slides around the meaning of events in order to place the self in a better light.* That which is good is labeled as of the self (internalization). Those qualities that are undesirable are excluded from the self by denial of their existence, disavowal of related attitudes, externalization, and negation of recent self-expressions. Persons who function as accessories to the self may also be idealized by exaggeration of their attributes. Those who counter the self are depreciated.

Such fluid shifts in meanings permit the narcissistic personality to maintain apparent logical consistency while minimizing "evil" or weakness and exaggerating innocence or control. As part of these maneuvers, the narcissistic personality may assume attitudes of contemptuous superiority toward others, emotional coldness, or even desperately charming approaches to idealized figures.

Reality-testing and reality-fantasy differentiation are not as readily lost in the narcissistic personality as in borderline or psychotic personalities. But the distorted meanings force further distortions as concealments. The resultant complications lend a subjectively experienced shakiness or uncertainty to ideational structures. Lapses in these defensive arrangements of ideas may occur during states of stress. Rages or paranoid states may occur, as may episodes of panic, shame, or depersonalization. Self-destructive acts may be motivated by wishes to end such pain, desires to harm the offending self, and the achievement of secondary gains such as obtaining sympathy or enacting a "wounded hero" role.

These various aspects of a prototypical narcissistic personality can be tabulated according to whether they are attributes of information-processing style, character traits, or habitual patterns of interpersonal relationships (see Table 8-1). The defensive style of sliding meanings, a central focus of this chapter, is only one of several defensive operations used to modulate new information to reduce threat. The argument can be made, as it has been by Shapiro (1965), that repetitious cognitive maneuvers, such as habitual use of sliding meanings, tend to lead to character traits and stereotyped forms of relationship. While further discussion of such a hypothesis is beyond the scope of this chapter, the defenses of patients are well known to be central concerns in psychoanalytic psychotherapy, and that alone justifies a closer look, even a detailed cognitive microanalysis, of this one operation.

To provide for such a cognitive analysis of a defensive operation it is useful to describe and diagram an ideational structure in which emotions are seen as responses to the match between sets of ideas, and potential emotional states are also seen as the motives for defensive maneuvers (Horowitz 1974a). To this end, a case vignette follows. This vignette has, in part, been used previously in Chapter 7 to model defensive operations in hysterical and obsessive personalities (Horowitz 1974b). The person, who is called Harry, is a fictitious elaboration of a real patient. He is used as a pliable model to maintain a constant state of symptomatology and conflict while varying theoretically the neurotic character style of the "patient." Thus the present

TABLE 8-1. Patterns in the Narcissistic Personality Style Prototype

Information-processing style

Short-order patterns—observe in flow of thought and emotion on a topic.

- Slides meanings of information that might damage self-concept.
  Also uses denial, disavowal, and negation for this purpose.
- Attention to sources of praise and criticism.
- Shifts subject-object focus of meanings, externalizes bad attributes, internalizes good attributes.
- Occasionally dissociates incompatible psychological attitudes into separate clusters.

Traits

Medium-order patterns—observe in interviews.

- Self-centered.
- Overestimates or underestimates self and others.
- Self-enhancement in accomplishments real or fantasied, in garb or demeanor.
- Avoids self-deflating situations.
- Variable demeanors depending on state of self-esteem and context:
  - charm, "wooing-winning" quality, controlling efforts, or charisma.
  - superiority, contemptuousness, coldness, or withdrawal.
  - shame, panic, helplessness, hypochondriasis, depersonalization, or self-destructiveness.
  - envy, rage, paranoia, or demands.

Interpersonal relations

Long-order patterns—observe in patient's history.

- Often impoverished interpersonally or oriented to power over others or controlling use of others as accessories (self-objects).
- Absence of "I-thou" feelings.
- Social climbing or using others for positive reflection.
- Avoidance of self-criticism by goading others to unfair criticism.
- Discarding of persons no longer of use.
- Pseudo twinning relationship.

Courtesy of Mardi J. Horowitz, *Stress Response Syndromes*.

analysis of a defense in a narcissistic Harry can be contrasted with the previous chapter on the cognitive analysis of switching in a compulsive Harry and inhibition in a histrionic Harry.

HARRY'S STORY RECAPITULATED

Harry was driving a truck down a highway late at night when he saw an attractive "hippie" girl hitch-hiking. He had the thought that she might be raped if he did not pick her up. In spite of the company rules against it, he accepted her as a passenger. Later, a car coming in the opposite direction crossed the divider strip. To avert a head-on collision, Harry drove off the road, and struck an obstacle. Awakening from a period of loss of consciousness, he found the girl's bloody body beside him. She was dead.

After a period of denial and numbing lasting several weeks, Harry began to have intrusive images of the girl's dead body both as nightmares and unbidden daytime images. He became irritable, suffered from insomnia, and began to drink far more than usual. With deterioration of his functional capacity, he was referred for psychotherapy.

During therapy, several conflictual themes activated by the accident emerged. Prominent among these were feelings of fear that he might have been killed, guilt over his own sexual ideas, guilt for "causing" her death, remorse for feeling relieved upon realizing he was alive and she was dead, and anger at her and the other driver for causing the accident. Of these various themes, worked through in different phases of the therapy, one is considered in what follows.

The presumed context, now, is the time in psychotherapy when Harry is talking about the intrusive images of the girl's body and the association between these images and ideas about his own vulnerability to death. Conceiving his possible death is incongruous with Harry's wishful attitude of invulnerability. The hazard of the incompatibility of these ideas is especially great for a narcissistic personality, since he has to maintain a brittle, but inviolately ideal, self-image.

Conceptually experienced, the incongruity tends to evoke fear beyond a level of toleration. Controls are instituted to prevent continuation or enlargement of such felt emotion. There is a double reason for such controls: to prevent the threatening levels of fear, and to avoid representation of fear, because it would also be a "narcissistic injury" for Harry to admit that he is scared. This "double jeopardy" of the narcissistic personality makes insight treatment difficult, as will be described shortly.

A microanalysis of the ideational-emotional structure begins, in State 1 of Figure 8-1, with the repetition of an image of the girl's dead body. This is the intrusive symptom Harry developed after the accident as part of a general compulsive repetition syndrome. The associated and responsive idea is that, since she is dead, he too might die. Personal vulnerability to death is grossly incongruous with an enduring concept of personal invulnerability, and this discrepancy evokes anxiety.

Defensive maneuvers are motivated by such signal anxiety. Subject designation is inhibited, leading to a more abstract idea, "someone dies," a less frightening concept than that the self may perish. By externalization and disavowal of the death construct, he slides the meaning of personal mortality into personal immortality, a version of undoing. Instead of anxiety, the shifts of

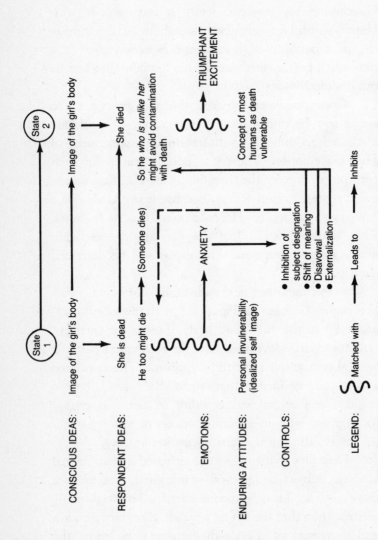

FIGURE 8-1 Microanalysis of the Ideational-Emotional Structure

CONSCIOUS IDEAS:

State 1 — Image of the girl's body
State 2 — Image of the girl's body

RESPONDENT IDEAS:

She is dead   She died
He too might die   So he who is unlike her
(Someone dies)   might avoid contamination
                     with death

EMOTIONS:

ANXIETY   TRIUMPHANT
                     EXCITEMENT

ENDURING ATTITUDES:

Personal invulnerability   Concept of most
(idealized self image)   humans as death
                                  vulnerable

CONTROLS:

• Inhibition of subject designation
• Shift of meaning
• Disavowal
• Externalization

LEGEND:

〰〰 Matched with   ──→ Leads to   ⇥→ Inhibits

meaning allow a sense of triumphant excitement by State 2. The very image that evoked anxiety now leads, by a slight irrationality, into a more positive emotional experience. State 2, because of its defensive nature, is essentially unstable, and Harry tends to repeat State 1.

The disavowal of any similarity between himself and the girl deserves a closer look. Narcissistic Harry exempts himself from group membership by thinking, in effect, "She is the kind who dies, I am not." To use an exaggerated version of this prototypical narcissistic defense, Harry classifies himself as an exception, perhaps with an extension of the idea that someone has to die. If someone has to die, then someone has been *chosen* to die, and it was she and not he. This then means he has been *saved* by this selection, presumably because he is special. Membership in the chosen group is like a sign of immortality; it is incongruent with the enduring concept of humans as vulnerable to death. This is a positive affect type of incongruity: things are better than anticipated. As diagrammed, Harry feels a kind of triumphant excitement in response to this set of ideas. Thus a complete reversal of emotions has been accomplished by shifting and undoing meanings and externalizing mortal contaminants such as death and vulnerability.

This sliding meanings maneuver is similar to an obsessional device in which one train of thought is used to block out another. But, unlike a prototypical obsessional, a narcissistic Harry experiences emotion, perhaps both fear and triumph. Also, the narcissistic Harry will not as readily go back and forth in endless undoing operations. In pure narcissistic form, he will not have to undo the triumph by feeling scared, even though he remains vulnerable to fear, and may repeat the sliding of meanings whenever fear-related ideas are reemergent.

TECHNIQUE IN
PSYCHOTHERAPY

How can a psychotherapist, once he or she has observed such defensive operations, deal with such fluid shifts in meaning? A useful counter in therapy is *reconstruction*, but tact in carrying this through is of great importance (Kohut 1971).

The narcissistic personality presents a double problem, as mentioned before. There is *both* the threat of warded-off ideas and experiences *and* the realization that he has been warding something off. Interpretations of defense and latent content are intolerable for narcissistic personalities unless they are tempered by proper dosage, timing, nuance of delivery, and the right kind of context in the therapeutic relationship. Otherwise the patient recognizes that he has distorted information in unrealistic ways and can have three traumas: (1) recognition of the self-threatening information, until then avoided by distortions; (2) shame that he needed to be told and was "caught" distorting something; and (3) a reactive need to give up the unrealistic but sustaining gratification of seeing himself as a person chosen by destiny for immortality.

Tact is also vital because, like the hysteric, the narcissistic personality may be more attentive to the therapist than to topical meanings. The therapist is an important current source of praise or criticism; the real or fantasied observation of the therapist's degree of interest will affect the patient's general equilibrium.

In the psychotherapy of a narcissistic Harry, during his expression and avoidance of the death themes just discussed, it would be helpful to recover and reconstruct the sequence of his fear of dying, including his memories of conceptual experiences during the accident. This procedure should be done as slowly as necessary to help Harry avoid a threat sufficient to throw him into a state of self-fragmentation.

During the reconstruction the therapist should also be unusually careful to obtain agreement as to Harry's self-experience as an instigator and an object. This is similar to the importance of scrutinizing activity and passivity in histrionic styles. Both therapist and patient would clarify how involved the patient was in every aspect of action: What was really his deed, and what happened for external reasons? This clarification would include discriminations between realities, real probabilities, and fantasies about his personal vulnerability. In the clarification and reconstruction some particular externalizations would be reversed, although the general tendency to externalization might not necessarily be interpreted.

For example, suppose a narcissistic Harry expresses rage at the other driver who forced him off the road. This externalizing of blame is an effort to symbolize to all that the fault lies with the other driver, not with Harry. Underlying this are not only threatening ideas of his realistic faults but unrealistic, potential accusations about his full culpability. The reconstruction involves every possible element of blame: how responsible is he for picking her up, for the cars in near collision, for pulling off the road in the way that he did, for actions after the crash? Some end point of realistic decision, reached for each topic, relieves Harry of the unrealistic components of blame. In the narcissistic personality these blame components are *not* necessarily an unconscious or conscious sense of guilt but rather criticisms that may come from any source and demolish self-esteem. The therapeutic action of review and reconstruction allows Harry to come to a conscious decision about his degree of culpability and allows him the experience of not being assaulted with criticism by the therapist (even when the therapist is goaded to make such assaults by the patient's flagrant externalizations).

Reconstructions and reviews will include the fear-evoking theme used for illustration. Working through this vulnerability theme will be especially difficult for narcissistic Harry. Realistic threats to self-integrity are his Achilles' heel, probably already lacerated by earlier traumas that may be revived and reopened in this context. Revivals of previous traumatic memories and fantasies, when seen, will also require reconstruction in the light of the present. These reconstructions with narcissistic patients need special extended efforts clarifying self and object distinctions about motives, beliefs, actions, and sensations.

During this process there will be shifts in topical meaning so that holding to a given aspect of a topic, as with obsessional patients, may be indicated. The nuance common with the narcissistic personality is to arrive at more stable meanings by encouraging the one meaning that has implications of current importance. For example, the "someone dies" idea has multiple meanings such as "each may die" or salvation of one through the "sacrificial death" of another. The grandiose idea of the sacrificial absolution is deflated by holding and discussing the more important fear themes around "each may die." If necessary, interpretation of the corrupted adherence to reality, as implied by the sacrifice-exemption theme, may be necessary but can be possible only if the therapeutic situation in some way provides adequate support for the patient's self-esteem.

NUANCES OF RELATIONSHIPS

Narcissistic considerations are present in every character type, not just narcissistic personality, and some of these nuances of treatment might be pertinent at any time. The "defects" commonly found in the typical narcissistic personality and comparable therapeutic counters are roughly summarized in Table 8-2.

Treatment of narcissistic personalities is often difficult for the therapist because the relationship with the patient is less invigorated by the real therapeutic alliance and the transference–countertransference colorations than with hysterical and obsessional patients. The narccisistic patient *uses* rather than *relates to* the therapist.

In spite of feeling unimportant as a real person, or distant, or bored, the therapist must understand what is going on and move tactfully closer to the patient. As with the hysterical patient in great stress, the therapist may have to be supportive for a period. With the narcissistic patient, support and closeness may not be so much a matter of warmth as a matter of accepting externalizations without interpretations. This will not be done without consequence, however, because later in therapy it will be necessary to interpret and discourage such externalizations.

The sense of safety necessary to experience and express usually warded-off ideas and feelings is achieved by the

TABLE 8-2. Some of the "Defects" of Narcissistic Style and Their Counteractants in Therapy

Function	Style as "defect"	Therapeutic counter
Perception	Focused on praise and blame	Avoid being provoked into either praising or blaming
	Denial of "wounding" information	Tactful timing and wording to counteract denials
Representation	Dislocates attributes as to whether of the self or another person	Clarify who is who in terms of acts, motives, beliefs, and sensations
Translation of images into words	Slides meanings	Consistently define meanings; encourage decisions as to most relevant meanings or weightings
Associations	Overbalanced in terms of finding routes to self-enhancement	Hold to other meanings; cautious deflation of grandiose meanings
Problem solving	Distortion of reality to maintain self esteem, obtain illusory gratifications, forgive self too easily	Point out corruptions (tactfully), encourage and reward reality-fidelity
		Support of self-esteem during period of surrender or illusory gratification (real interest of therapist and identification with therapist as noncorrupt person)
		Help develop appropriate sense of responsibility
		Find out and discourage unrealistic gratification from therapy

Courtesy of Mardi J. Horowitz, *Stress Response Syndromes.*

narcissistic personality through two types of quasi-relationship. One form is characterized by personal grandiosity, with the expectation of admiration, the other by idealizing the therapist, with the expectation of security because of the relationship with an ideal figure (Kohut 1971).

The grandiose quasi-relationship will tend to occur either at the beginning of treatment or during recovery from an initially defeated state of mind precipitated by the stress event. Bragging and self-endorsements will occur in subtle or gross forms and take time away from stress-relevant topics. Tact, as emphasized earlier, will take the form of allowing these efforts to restore self-esteem, rather than insisting upon staying with core conflicts or interpreting the grandiose effort as compensatory.

This tact and forbearance may be unusually difficult for therapists who are used to relying on the therapeutic alliance or positive transference to tide the patient over periods of hard work on threatening ideas. It is difficult to remember that the relationship with narcissistic patients is not stable and that their need is imperative but not coordinated with the usual concerns, however ambivalent, for the person upon whom they direct their needs.

In the second common form of quasi-relationship, idealizing the therapist, the repair of damage is effected by the patient's imagining that he is once again protected and given worth by a powerful or attractive parent. The stress response syndrome becomes a ticket of admission for this kind of self-supplementation. Again, tactful tolerance is necessary early in the treatment, when the person is still partially overwhelmed by the stress response syndrome. It would be an error to see behavior such as exaggerated testimonials to the therapist's unique ability as equivalent to the transference-motivated seduction gambits of some hysterical patients or the undoing of negative feelings on the part of obsessional patients. The testimonials simply indicate idealization, which provides a momentary repair of damage to the self, a safer time during which some work on processing and integrating stress events may occur.

Even externalizations can help a patient gain sufficient emotional distance from loaded topics to tolerate thinking about them. For example, if a feeling of disgust about death is projected onto the therapist, the relevant nuance would be to ask the patient to talk further about how the therapist feels. This allows the patient to work along the ideational routes as if it were the therapist's route. A direct interpretation, such as "You are disgusted by death," should only come later.

REFERENCES

Adler, A. (1916). *The Neurotic Constitution: Outlines of a Comparative Individualistic Psychology and Psychotherapy*. Trans. B. Gluck and J. Lind. New York: Moffat Yard and Co.

Buber, M. (1878). *I and Thou*. 2nd ed. Trans. R. G. Smith. New York: Charles Scribners Sons, 1958.

Freud, S. (1914). On narcissism: an introduction. *Standard Edition* 14:69–102.

_____ (1920). Beyond the pleasure principle. *Standard Edition* 18:7–64.

Furst, S. S. (1967). Psychic trauma: a survey. In *Psychic Trauma*, ed. S. S. Furst, pp. 3–50. New York: Basic Books.

Horowitz, M. J. (1973). Phase oriented treatment of stress response syndromes. *American Journal of Psychotherapy* 27:506–515.

_____ (1974a). Microanalysis of working through in psychotherapy. *American Journal of Psychiatry* 131:1208–1212.

_____ (1974b). Stress response syndromes: character style and brief psychotherapy. *Archives of General Psychiatry* 131:768–781.

Kernberg, O. (1966). Structural derivatives of object relationships. *International Journal of Psycho-Analysis* 47:236–253.

_____ (1970). Factors in the psychoanalytic treatment of narcissistic personalities. *Journal of the American Psychoanalytic Association* 18:51–85.

_____ (1974). Further contributions to the treatment of narcissistic personalities. *International Journal of Psycho-Analysis* 55:215–240.

Kohut, H. (1966). Forms and transformations of narcissism. *Journal of the American Psychiatric Association* 14:243–272.

_____ (1968). The psychoanalytic treatment of narcissistic personality disturbances. *Psychoanalytic Study of the Child* 23:86–113.

_____ (1971). *The Analysis of the Self*. New York: International Universities Press.

_____ (1972). Thoughts on narcissism and narcissistic rage. *Psychoanalytic Study of the Child* 27:360–400.

Mahler, M. (1968). *On Human Symbiosis and the Vicissitudes of Individuation*. New York: International Universities Press.

Shapiro, D. (1965). *Neurotic Styles*. New York: Basic Books.

Cognitive Structure and Change in the Histrionic Personality

The goal of this chapter is to describe a method for writing case histories in a manner that mediates between simple description of the analytic process and the abstract generalizations of metapsychology. This intermediate level involves the development of inferences that define cognitive process and schematic structure. In particular, there is definition of the principal ways that defenses operate to distort information-processing of the main self and object schemata that organize information and guide behavior. With such definition it is possible to describe modification during the course of analysis of those cognitive operations of a defensive and resistive nature, and of basic self and object schemata that color the transference.

To achieve these ends, a typical case of hysterical* character is described. The history of the analysis is given and followed by formulations from the six metapsychological points of view. The cognitive and schematic points of view are then discussed in detail, with a focus on learning during the analysis.

BACKGROUND

Psychoanalysis provides profound data about psychological dynamics and the processes of change during treatment. The perennial problem has been the systematization of this data (Horowitz 1987, Knapp 1974, Wallerstein and Sampson 1971). If the dynamics and the processes of change can be described clearly, then this knowledge will in turn supply solutions to two pressing psychiatric riddles: the understanding of varieties of psychopathology of character and the process of change in psychotherapy. If the change processes in psychoanalysis, the most extensive of all treatment forms, can be understood for a given character typology, then this knowledge would allow a clear

---

*I have maintained for this reading the original usage of "hysterical" as a qualitative descriptor of a character prototype. This was the tem in use when this contribution was written, and it is interchangeable with the term "histrionic."

stance for consideration of a methodology for shorter forms of treatment to approach and modify equivalent situations.

Metapsychological points of view provide a framework for considering causative factors in an overdetermined psychological system (Rapaport and Gill 1959). Unfortunately, the metapsychological level of abstraction is far removed from clinical observations and inferences (Gedo et al. 1964, Peterfreund 1971). More detailed explanations are indicated, such as those described for the modification of defense (Sampson et al. 1972, Weiss, 1967, 1971). Describing modification of self and object representations is another important task, emphasized by Jacobson (1954, 1964), Kernberg (1966, 1970), Kohut (1968, 1971), and Schafer (1968).

COGNITIVE POINT OF VIEW

In terms of cognitive process it is necessary to describe habitual styles of ideation, emotion, and defense, such as those described as "neurotic styles" by Shapiro (1965). An explanation of defenses is central to this task since defenses are ways of warding off or distorting information from within the mind or from external sources. Repression and denial were the defenses used most extensively by the patient to be described. While repression was her favored mode of warding off mental contents and emotional reactions, one still needs to understand how this was accomplished in terms of her characteristic manner of perception, attention deployment, representation, association, and serial organization of thought. In terms of cognitive structure it is necessary to describe the initial state and subsequent alteration of her basic schemata of self and object relationships. Modification of process is necessary to accomplish such modifications of self and object representation. Such structural change then allows further change in process because previously intolerable emotional states can be experienced. Further process changes structure further, and so on in a transactive series that is the central topic of this chapter.

Because an important aspect of the discussion of change will focus on self and object relationships, it is important to distinguish between self and object *images*, *representations*, and *schemata*. These terms are used variously in the psychological, British and American psychoanalytic literature; therefore, working definitions for this paper will be given.

A self or object *image* will mean an episode of experience in sensory form that can be quite short in time. A self or object *representation* will refer to an experienced organization of information that may also be quite short. Unlike "image," the mode of representation is not necessarily sensory. One can have a self-representation by words describing the self. The word *schemata* will be reserved for enduring organizers of information about the self or objects. What Jacobson (1964) calls self-representations may here be called self schemata, a term used to describe a slowly changing blueprint about the self.

CASE HISTORY

Miss Smith was 25 years old when she came for treatment. Slender, well formed, and very attractive, she had striking black hair and eyebrows and a very pale face. She said she came because she felt depressed and unsure of how to continue her life.

While recently deserted by a lover, her depressed feelings were not simply reactive grief. She recognized a recurrent pattern of failure in all her relationships. She was troubled by anorgasmia, anxieties on first contacts with men, and an inability to let herself love. Her loneliness was increased by an absence of friendships.

At the onset of treatment Miss Smith was in a final year of internship before obtaining a credential as a dietician. This apprenticeship was going poorly. On some days instead of going to work, she stayed in her bed at the boarding house where she lived. She felt too dizzy, lightheaded, and apathetic to rise, and was uncertain whether her illness was physical or psychological. Phobias, dissociative episodes, and conversion symptoms were occasionally present, but she did not report them until later in the analysis.

On evaluation she reported another motive for treatment and reason for depression. Her older sister had recently had a baby. Even if she were to be cured of sexual inhibitions and inability to love, she could not marry and bear children in time to "catch up."

Most of the complaints present at the onset of analysis were relieved by the time analysis was completed. The plan to prepare this chapter was discussed with the patient more than a year after termination. The symptomatic improvements indicated for the time of termination had persisted. She had made a fine advancement in a rewarding career and felt successful in what she did. She was as yet unmarried but able to relate tenderly and orgastically to men. She felt that "analysis was the best thing she had ever done and that it was astounding in view of how she was before and after." She found that problems came up in everyday life, but she was coping well with them.

Her background: Miss Smith's mother was rigid and moralistic. Her family found her joyless and often depressed.
Devoted to the Catholic Church, she served on its committee on pornography, and was concerned throughout
life with social propriety. Her origin as the child of lower
middle-class parents meant that her marriage to Mr.
Smith, son of a once prominent family, indicated upward
mobility. She seemed as proud of that as she was
ashamed by Mr. Smith's vocational and social failures.

Mrs. Smith was trained in a semi-professional skill.
After her first pregnancy she stayed home as housewife
and mother. The patient was born two years later, to be
followed in two more years by a third daughter. This
third child had mild congenital deformities and was also
susceptible to viral diseases and allergies. Reconstruction
and family stories suggest that the mother had a depres-
sive episode after this last pregnancy. Her infirmities and
those of her latest baby kept Mrs. Smith from returning
to work, although finances then were meager. When the
children entered school, she returned to work at a large
military base where, because of her great work productivity, efficiency, and self-effacing nature, she rapidly
gained a position of semi-executive responsibility.

The first daughter was lively and spunky. She
began promiscuous sexual activities early in adolescence
and demonstrated an average intelligence. The patient,
the second child, was quieter, more intelligent, and
well-behaved. The third child was sickly, less intelligent
than the other two, and received a great deal of nursing
care from the mother.

Mrs. Smith became obese and Miss Smith found
her coarse and unappealing. The mother's only hobby
was reviewing magazines for obscene content so that they
might be banned by the church. She hid these magazines
in her lingerie drawer, an open secret in the family. The

proud moralistic stance of the mother was brittle. Sometimes she wept uncontrollably over conflicts within the family. At such times she felt helpless and complained of being unappreciated. She also felt insecure in public. For example, when returning a purchase at a department store, she would use the two older girls, when they were adolescents, to front for her.

Mr. Smith was unusual. All of his daughters regarded him as a failure and a sexual pervert but also knew him to be artistically gifted and capable of enthusiasm. One of his greatest eccentricities was nudism. He insisted upon practicing his nudity around the house, including taking his breakfast while naked. He assumed the function of waking each daughter and would lie undressed on their beds, above the covers, until they arose. During early adolescence this so embarrassed and upset the patient that she begged her mother to make him stop. Her mother would cry and claim that she was helpless.

Mr. Smith, while selfish and immature, could be lively and endearing. He drew well and would amuse the children with cartoons. He might take the patient for a ride in the car, thrilling her by turns at high speed. Ideal images of her father had their disappointing side, however. When he was obviously and repeatedly cheated by mechanics and used-car dealers, his aura of expertise with cars was demolished. Mr. Smith had graduated with honors in art history from a major university. He then found an unusually good job as assistant curator of an art museum but was let go at the end of one year. After a sequence of false starts he became a pigment tester for a line of paints, going from factory to factory to assure quality control. The salary was low, and he was regarded as a failure.

While the father overtly chided his oldest daughter for her sexual behavior, covertly he was interested and teased for details. Later, when Miss Smith was in college, he wanted to visit her to flirt with her roommate. There were other episodes of his flirtations with women such as waitresses. These were pathetic longings without action. While he ridiculed the smut committee, he surreptitiously read the pornographic material from her mother's drawer. At times he masturbated so that sounds could be overheard, or left his fly unzipped in public. These exhibitionistic traits were limited. He was never apprehended in a flagrant act.

Together, the parents set a familial standard of denial and rationalization. Granted this background, it is not surprising that arousal, anger, anxiety, and guilt over erotic events characterized Miss Smith's childhood. Her older sister encouraged her to strip before a group of boys 9 to 13 years old, when she was about four or five years old. When she removed her panties she was roundly laughed at. Later, a boy she had especially admired from afar asked her to his room. He showed her an obscene photograph and she rushed out. Striptease was a favored game of the oldest sister and the three girls often played it.

She commenced menstruation when she was nine years old. She was surprised at the blood, having had no preparation. Her sister, who was eleven, was supportive, although her own periods had not yet begun. When the mother came home she assumed the menses to be painful and put the patient to bed. The older sister reached menarche shortly thereafter. Unlike the patient, her breasts and pubic hair began to grow. The patient assumed her own breasts would never grow, and the sister encouraged her in this belief.

The oldest sister went on to flagrant promiscuous activities, which the parents deplored, but did not stop. The patient remained a quiet and withdrawn adolescent, devoted to religion and books. She daydreamed of boys but was afraid of them. She went to the earliest mass to avoid the shame of being seen with her family. In church she imagined herself recognized as especially good and spiritual, and relished the eventual damnation of her sister. It would be she who would be rescued by an ideal lover, marry, and have children she would love and bring up properly.

Miss Smith was sent to a religious prep school where she boarded. She felt miserably homesick, but was only allowed home on some weekends. She hoped that her spiritual goodness would result in recognition from peers and teachers and was very disappointed. The socially prominent girls were better groomed and dressed, and more appealing to teachers in spite of their various sexual adventures with boys.

All three sisters had little social poise. Role models at home made ideal identifications difficult. The older sister learned by experience and matured into an interesting and vivacious person. She dated a series of men, and then married one whom the patient felt to be outstanding. This marriage proved sound, and the sister continued to develop into a warm and compassionate woman. The failure of damnation of this sister for her earlier promiscuity was the central cause of the patient's later alteration in religious beliefs. Meanwhile the youngest sister was plagued by difficulties. She lived at home even after graduation from high school, held marginal jobs, and had an impoverished social life.

While drastically limited in social activities, Miss Smith did well academically in private school and was accepted into a good college. Wealth in the father's family, withheld from him personally, provided a trust fund for her education and later life. Her mother suggested that she major in economics since it could lead to a glamorous life in the world of finance. Not knowing what else to do, she followed this suggestion. During the first years she felt insecure and somewhat fraudulent when she got good grades. Neither of the other sisters was able to complete college, but Miss Smith did not feel superior or knowledgeable.

Dramatically, one day in church, she decided God did not exist and that her restraint from sexual activity was wasted. With a sense of anger, but no particular plan, she allowed herself to be seduced by a man she admired, who was president of her church group. She then fantasied they were engaged. When he married someone else, she was surprised and dismayed. Only then did she begin to masturbate, with accompanying feelings of guilt and anxiety.

On completion of college she obtained an unusually good job in a banking corporation, one which actually had the romantic component of travel. She did satisfactory work but felt that she was only pretending to be capable. Contacts with co-workers frightened her. She gradually assumed a façade of poise and glamour, and entered into two affairs. In the first, she was clearly used and then dropped. The second seemed like the love she sought. Although she supported the young man financially, he seemed "on the way up." Again, while nothing had been said, she assumed they were engaged. He walked out on her, and she felt bitter and depressed.

At this crisis point Miss Smith was determined to reorganize herself. She recognized a continued lack of pleasure in sexual intercourse and felt fraudulent at work. She decided to change her position and to learn actively about sex. She selected nutrition as a field and entered graduate school with the aim of becoming a dietician in a large medical center. While she did not seek out particular men, she entered into fortuitous affairs. These were uniformly unsatisfying and brief.

Attractive, personable, and successful young men were too overwhelming. Instead she tended to meet either older men or younger men who were ineligible for marriage. Courtship rituals with their slow explorations were also too anxiety-provoking. Undressing together, especially slowly, was particularly threatening. She preferred to get into bed as quickly as possible, feeling that the relationship could be more friendly and "less frantic" after intercourse. The men she became involved with fell into two distinct patterns in a personal pecking order. Men of "lower" status might be successful financially but were either less attractive or much older than she. Men of "higher" status were younger and as good-looking as she was, but were ineligible and hence tolerable because of some other feature.

In the affairs with younger men she was generally a used and abused person. She would submit to rapid intercourse, then expect to be taken out, especially to good restaurants, and showed off. Instead, she would be driven home, or lend the lover money, or clean his apartment, or perform some other submissive task. She was unable to reveal, much less assert or insist upon, her own desires. Her one aggressive move was to reveal her frigidity, usually at some later point in the relationship. This challenge sometimes made men try very hard to get her to achieve a climax. They were never successful.

Older or lower-status men would fall in love with her, treat her tenderly, give her gifts. Then the glamorous, free, uninhibited swinger role that she initially played in every affair would rapidly deteriorate. She felt apathetic and deadened in their presence. The only remaining excitement was in deciding when and how she would reveal this to them and stop seeing them. To avoid breaking their hearts, the affair might be protracted with futile attempts on their part to be of more interest.

She would eventually challenge any man's virility by relevation of his inability to bring her to orgasm. Every affair ended in disaster. Either she was hurt or she hurt some man. Her hopes for marriage and children grew dim. Sexual freedom and sensual pleasure did not come with sexual experience. Her graduate work entered the phase of internship and this began to go poorly as interpersonal contacts were demanded.

A final affair seemed unusually promising and she fantasied marriage until the man abruptly left her, culminating her depression over a lack of progress in any area of her life. Someone she knew had been greatly helped by psychotherapy and she decided to consult this person's therapist. The extent of her difficulties, together with her strong motivation and intelligence, prompted that therapist to refer her for consideration of psychoanalysis.

COURSE OF ANALYSIS

First year

During the evaluation hours Miss Smith presented herself as vivacious, earnest, intelligent, and compliant. She asked many questions and requested little favors such as telephone usage, car fare, and time changes. During the first sessions, after a decision for a trial of analysis, her grooming was less meticulous, her demeanor more anxious. She was more childlike, had periods of silence, and wanted to be instructed or prodded on how to continue.

This initial series of hours was used by her to test the analyst's response to provocations. When he was neither too reactive to attention-getting devices nor too responsive to demands for support, she began talking of current difficulties at work and in a new love affair. This most recent affair was begun impulsively, coincident with the onset of treatment and was seen later as a defensive maneuver to prevent a positive transference. She had read about analysis and felt she was expected to fall in love with her therapist. She thought this preposterous, an indication of the eccentric ideas the therapist probably held, and the last thing that would ever happen however much the analyst might try to evoke such feelings.

In any topical context she continued to try the analyst, to see if he would respond erratically when she was provocative, comfort her when she was upset, or pursue her when she was distant. This pattern was repetitive, at increasingly clearer levels of awareness, throughout most of the treatment period. After weeks of these episodes, she entered the room late and distraught. Obviously shaken, she stood dramatically against the door and announced that she had come only to say goodbye, that she could not go on with analysis because, among other things, she could not tolerate lying on the couch.

She agreed to talk this over and spent several sessions sitting in a chair. The constant neutrality and "coolness" of the analyst reassured her, but she complained bitterly that she needed tranquilizers and counseling. She continued analysis, resumed use of the couch, but felt extremely depressed. She spent mornings in bed and avoided her internship duties. She then had to take a leave of absence from school to avoid being officially dropped, began three affairs at once and risked pregnancy. She had stopped birth-control pills because of side effects but was too frightened of gynecologists to request a diaphragm.

During the analytic hours she demanded and pleaded for help. She found it hard to verbalize her ideas and feelings and wanted the analyst to disclose his personal weaknesses so that she would know it was all right to reveal hers. She reported many other kinds of treatment in which therapists were more revealing, kinder, more giving, faster, and better. She admitted that she consciously withheld information and reports of current events. The analyst's response to these various maneuvers was to clarify what she was saying, largely by repetition. For example, with transference issues he might say, "You want me to do something more active to help you," or "You don't think you can stand it if I just keep listening and telling you what I think is going on." With outside issues, the analyst attempted to clarify patterns of interaction and cause and effect. Again, the style involved short repetitions of what she had said and occasional requests for more detail.

Miss Smith began to reveal indirect sexual fantasies of the analyst in dreams and daydreams but denied their implications. She developed a phobia of walking on the street near the office with a specific theme of fear of being seen by the analyst. This phobia generalized to a fear of riding buses, because people might look at her.

She continued to insist that she badly needed sexual advice, support, and warmth but was not getting it. Her wishes that she be counseled in sexual technique closely paralleled her most frequently used masturbation fantasy.

In that fantasy, she imagined a girl lying on an examining table. A nurse told her that the doctor was examining her and that the procedure was done for medical reasons, was quite safe, and had nothing to do with sex. It was implied that later the doctor would gradually and carefully explain all kinds of details about sexual intercourse. The doctor, in the visual images of the fantasy, was scarcely present and the girl was only vaguely herself.

In spite of her demands to be given more, she reacted in an almost startled manner to many statements by the analyst. She episodically insisted that his clarifications were forcing her to go too far. The analyst and psychoanalysis were alternately boring and weird, orthodox and decadent, pushing her too fast and not helping at all. Nonetheless, towards the end of the year, she was working rather hard on clarifying many important life patterns and getting a first approximation of their meanings. A turning point, perhaps equal in importance to her not leaving analysis when frightened, was her rejection of a marriage proposal made by a wealthy, attractive, young man who would have taken her away to another country. The proposal reenacted one of her favorite fantasies and her reluctance to accept it signaled recognition of the deep-seated and, thus far, unresolved nature of her characterological problems.

She began to accept confrontations and clarifications about her global denials, childlike establishment of simple rules (a form of rationalization), and abrupt cessation of topics. As her life patterns became clear, they seemed very sad to her and she became depressed. A one-month vacation by the analyst deepened this depression. She stated she had made the wrong choice when she decided to continue analysis and "might go crazy" during the free interval.

She berated the returning analyst for deserting her. At the same time she began to bring up pertinent memories from childhood in which she had experienced similar feelings from maternal deprivations. Her envy of her older sister, who was able to "get away" from the family, and of her younger sister, who received special care within the family, also emerged. Her angry wishes that this older sister be punished for her sexual activities were associated with her hitherto unconscious guilt over her own sexual acts. The wish to be like her sick younger sister and deserve special and continuous attention also emerged and was connected to similar feelings of yearning for attention from the analyst.

Her wishes emerged clearly in a dream. She had "gone crazy," and the analyst was thus forced to take care of her "properly" by bringing her to live in his home-sanatorium. The scene was of a white columned mansion, surrounded by tranquil lawns, with therapy conducted beside a swimming pool. Special amongst a group of women patients, she would lie along the diving board, as if asleep, and receive tender care.

Second year

The anniversary of one year of analysis led to a renewed period of depression. She had heard that special patients finished in one year and was disappointed. She reacted by setting a termination date one year hence. She found it intolerable to think of analysis lasting any longer than that. She made increased efforts at self observation and at free association. Guarded enthusiasm about understanding herself and gaining control of her behavior led to an increasingly evident transference neurosis in which she tried to ward off sexual interest, anxiety, and guilt.

Various arousing and traumatic childhood memories were reported, such as her fearful fascination as she was allowed to watch her father shave off his pubic hair. She expected the analyst to be enthusiastic about such revelations, because they would prove his eccentric psychoanalytic theories. While she discounted the meaning of such memories, she both feared and expected that they would lead to fervid cooperation on analytic work, lyrical excitement, and then a carried-away sexual transport by both parties during the treatment hour.

Trying out these ideas in relatively clear language without such results gave her an increased sense of safety. With a lessened fear of intimacy and also as a resistance to the transference, she became closer to one of two concurrent male friends. Her exploitation and rescue fantasies were clarified. While trying out greater freedom, she developed anxiety attacks when with her male friend or en route to the treatment hours.

Once again preoccupied with the analysis and the analyst, she decided to give up her male friends until she was cured of her sexual inhibitions. She masturbated more and began work on her recurrent masturbation fantasies. She recognized her inhibitions against representing men, penises, or vaginas even in her private fantasies. Then the woman nurse figure became a primary sexual object. Although she was afraid of becoming a homosexual, she threatened the analyst by stating her intentions to experiment with homosexuality if he did not hurry and cure her frigidity with men. Her main homosexual fantasies were a wish to stare at large breasts and sexualized wishes for nurturance at the breast.

When the threat of homosexuality did not evoke a nonanalytic response from the therapist, and while under pressure from the clarification and interpretation of the transference meanings of these threats, she again carried her testing of the analytic situation to an extreme. She "got" raped by walking on the beach in a lonely area after dark, started several new affairs, and then threatened suicide during the depression that resulted when these impulsive relationships ended badly.

Following this turbulent period there was marked reduction in denial and repression. Sexual ideas towards the analyst were spoken of clearly and linked to childhood memories of relationships with her father. The emotional responses were more fully developed and were experienced as tolerable levels of anxiety, depression, and guilt, rather than as emotional storms.

Third year

The third year could be summarized as a working through of father and mother transference neuroses in the context of the therapeutic alliance. While interpretation of resistances remained a prominent technique, her responses were different. Instead of denial and repression, she changed her defensive operations. She used dreams, free associations, and recollections well, accepted and helped with reconstructions, and experienced and reported bodily sensations and feeling states as they fluctuated during the hour. Instead of global depressions she felt sad and disappointed about specific aspects of her life.

In general, she moved from a passive to an active stance. She had been working as a secretary after dropping out of her postgraduate training. She was now able to get a paramedical job on the basis of her partial training as a dietician and to reapply to school.

With continued work on her defective body image, avoidance of ideas about sex, inhibitions of arousal, and fear of altered consciousness during intercourse, she began to enjoy sexual activities with men. Her first orgasm occurred during mutual masturbation; she then became orgastic during intercourse. There were still difficulties, however, and fuller erotic experiences were not achieved until after a termination date was set some time later.

With increased freedom in heterosexual activities and fantasies, her free-floating anxiety attacks changed into phobic forms. For example, after experimenting with fellatio for the first time, she feared that an ordinary facial pimple was a syphilitic canker sore. Her aggressive and castrating impulses towards men also emerged into clear representational expression. She wanted to control the man's penis, or at least govern, in an exaggerated way, when it would or would not enter her body. Without such control she feared her body would be hurt.

This fear of being hurt was reasonable in view of her childlike body image. As she was able to think and communicate more clearly, she could reveal that her self image did not include a vaginal opening. During intercourse she had been numb in the pelvic area, although feelings were possible during masturbation. Now she was able to explore herself and use words to label genital parts. The "nonexistent area" in her body image went through stages; first, of cloacal chaos in which her vagina and rectum were imagined as coalesced, and then a sense of a separate, inadequate but discrete vagina about two inches in length.

Not surprisingly, pregnancy fantasies emerged in dreams, then in daydreams and reverie. Her masturbation fantasies evolved in a progression. First she imagined herself as a vague child-woman, then as a man, being the one in control and telling a virgin about pelvic examinations and then sex. Next, repeating the homosexual phase of the previous year, she imagined herself as a woman doing things to another woman, and finally herself as a woman being fondled by a very gentle reassuring man.

This work led to intensification of the sexualized transference neurosis. She became frightened by her emotional experience during therapy hours. She fantasied that she would cry so much she could never stop, or else that the analyst would be so moved that the love affair would at last become irresistible. Alternate exhibitionistic and voyeuristic impulses were clarified and related to her phobias and to various recalled experiences with both parents.

Fourth year

While a mixture of yearning, frustration, hostility, and disgust towards her mother had emerged episodically throughout the analysis, particularly emotional memories about her now occupied center stage. Entwined with these memories were her envy of both sisters, the jealousy and thwarted competitive urges towards her older sister, and resentment for the attentive ministrations received by the younger sister. She worked through several patterns of relationships between herself and other women, both historically and in the present, as well as those mirrored currently in the analytic situation.

In one of these configurations she was the poor, passive, helpless victim of the hostility and lack of concern of her mother, the analyst, or an older woman. At other times she remained a helpless victim, but the other person was not so much an aggressor as simply insufficient. An idealized masculine rescuer was, in a life script on the order described by Berne (1961), supposed to find and care for her at this point. As a child of about 4 or 5 years of age her father did fulfil this role, taking her for car rides to cheer her up. Her ideal version of him was later displaced by disillusionment but remained as a configuration of hope for another hero.

In another configuration, she at last unleashed the destructive reactions to her disappointments. Much to her great surprise, embarrassment, anxiety, guilt, and pleasure, she was able to tongue-lash the analyst. She had fantasies of shooting him, of blowing up his car, and feared visiting her parents because she would tear the lid off their hypocrisies and denials. Once again, the analysis was a dangerous provocation and could be responsible for any mayhem she might commit.

As she was able to tolerate the experience of strong feelings without a sense of losing control, the various representations of herself in relation to members of her family were described, reviewed, and reconsidered with increasing clarity. Using her adult mind, she was able to compare memories and fantasies with one another. Compartmentalization of good and bad images of each important person was reduced, and she had feelings of "realization" about people. For example, she was deeply moved by being able to remember her father as having both good and bad qualities. He was interesting, sincere, aesthetic, even powerful at times while also neurotic, infantile, perverse, seductive, and unreliable.

Her self representations had also changed as therapy progressed, but now these changes were more clearly delineated. There was a period of conscious alteration in her sense of her body and her identity. She had fantasies and dreams of the analyst's wife, a person she had never heard of or seen, but presumed existed. The wife was imagined variously as her mother, sisters, and ego ideal. First, the wife was imagined as a flamboyant mistress type, named "Titsy." She also fantasied the wife as sickly or fat, and herself as a yearned-for substitute. Then the wife image in dreams changed to a mature, attractive, concerned woman who spoke kindly to her. In one dream in which she, the patient, had come to the analyst's home and was uneasy about how appropriate the visit might be, the wife told her it was all right and talked sociably with her. Miss Smith identified, in a comparatively deliberate way, with these idealized projections. She allowed herself to continue complaining about her own mother, to feel sad that her mother would never change, and again to fantasize being the child of the analyst and his wife.

During this period Miss Smith changed her style of grooming and dress to one that seemed somehow to "fit" her personality. She experienced guilt at entering a different league from her mother, especially as she was now able to meet and get to know "men with suits." Finally, she had feelings of "reality" about her mother, and was able to accept her limitations. During the first part of the analysis she had been remote from her parents. During the third year she had visited them and returned disappointed. In view of her own altered impressions of them and feelings of control, she had expected a magical change in them that would make them capable of more intimate relationships with her. Now, when she visited them again, she felt that she could accept them as they were. She no longer felt the need to accuse them, nor was she disappointed by the limitations still imposed on her relationships with them.

Her sexual fantasies continued to shift and she felt more open towards both the physical and emotional components of relating to men. She also began to have experiences of "reality" which were simply keen perceptions with knowledge of what was going on. She felt as if her body parts and those of her sexual partner were real, and this surprised her. She recognized a residual fear of enthusiasm in sex and linked this to her fear of enthusiasm in the analysis. Resistance was generally absent and major interpretive efforts seemed unnecessary as the work progressed by itself, as it were.

She felt in control of her life, effective, able to think and feel, to work out her own solutions to everyday life problems. Ideas of transience, life ending in death, aging and menopause occurred and filled her with sadness. Then she discussed ideas of terminating the analysis. After several emergences and avoidances of this idea, a termination date half a year ahead was agreed upon. She then experienced this date-setting as an unfair trick and a loss of interest. The ending was ill-timed, she felt, because, while her symptoms were gone and her life was in control, she had neither married and had a child nor embarked securely on her profession. A series of transference repetitions occurred in which the analyst was compared to the uncaring mother. Gratified by his fine performance in curing her, the analyst now no longer cared what she might or might not do, and planned to get rid of her before giving her everything. On the other hand, he was also like the tricky, eccentric father. The termination was a way to confront her with her residual problems, or perhaps a device that would lead to a postanalytic love tryst. These reactions were readily translated into words and understanding, with toleration and working through of related emotions and memories. At the end, she felt a little sad that she had lost some interest in the analysis and was very grateful for the results of the work. She had occasional fears of relapse, but according to the follow-up mentioned earlier, these fears proved unfounded.

THE PROCESSES OF CHANGE

The clinical inferences about Miss Smith can now be reviewed in terms of basic patterns both before and at end of treatment. Changes in these patterns will be considered first in terms of the customary metapsychological points of view, then in terms of cognitive psychology, which is subsidiary to the structural point of view. Discussing the six metapsychological points of view one by one leads to such redundancy that they have been combined into three compatible pairs: the developmental and adaptational, the structural and topographic, and the economic and dynamic points of view.

Development and adaptation

In the hierarchical model of metapsychology suggested by Gedo and Goldberg (1973), Miss Smith would be seen as beginning the analysis in Phase IV, i.e., the stage of psycho-sexual and psychosocial development in which the main hazards are moral anxiety over incestuous and aggressive object-related strivings. Her principal defenses, repression and denial, developed because of a cognitive preparedness for such modes at the developmental stage, her internaliza-tion of the family practice of utilizing these defenses in communication, and the amenable nature of the main threats to such controls. Her characterological develop-ment was also colored by a pregenital ambivalent attach-ment to her mother.

By this oedipal period of childhood development, Miss Smith had successfully differentiated herself as separate from her mother, and she had a clear gender identification as a female. But precursors of adult female sexuality, such as flirtatiousness and display, were warded off, leaving a par-tially nonintegrated and partially defective childlike self schemata that was not revised because everyday forms of sexual self images and representations were warded off. In general, this was done to avoid guilt over sexual excitement and anxiety over her fear of sexual assault. With analysis, these warding-off maneuvers were interpreted and counter-acted. The childlike and defective self schemata were repro-cessed in terms of conscious experience of current self images and representations. She was gradually able to integrate female genitalia into her self schemata, leading to increased confidence in her capacity for sexual relations.

In addition to this progression towards completion of the genital phase of psychosexual development, Miss Smith had persistent conflicts from the oral phase (Easser and Lesser 1965, Marmor 1953, Zetzel 1970). Strong yearnings to be nurtured, literally and symbolically, were associated, unconsciously, with a magical belief that someone always suffered when such desires were present. Either she would suck dry and deplete her mother, as her mother virtually told her she had done, or she was deliberately neglected as unworthy of concern. These oral-aggressive components of this complex of ideas and feelings extended into a blurred anal-sadistic dimension in which she wanted to let go of her feelings but feared a disastrous loss of control. The fear of loss of sphincter control colored her genital development, leading to explicit fears of bowel or bladder mishaps if enthusiastic sexual responses were to occur. Guilt over destructive aims coupled with the fear of loss of control served to render the negative affect and negative schemata of mother highly hazardous.

Analytic work instigated the conscious processing of these variegated and blurred-together themes. She was able to differentiate sexual strivings from oral wishes to be comforted and caressed. Her impulsivity in sexual relationships was attenuated once she could seek what she wanted at any particular time without confusion of aims, and could accept partial gratification. She came to recognize when she was enraged over frustration and how she warded off the emergence of such anger.

Her oedipal *fantasies* were integrated with an unusual frequency of *real life events*. Her father was sexually provocative in his exhibitionism and there was a real impairment in the mother-father relationship. Any fantasy she might entertain in conscious awareness was difficult to isolate from memories or expectations of real occurrences.

Her self–object schemata at the onset of analysis concretized an internalized version of these familial patterns into a set of stereotyped roles. These roles, to be described

later in detail, were imposed compulsively on every relationship. Real experiences were held at such great distance,
by nonappraisal of meanings and general denial, that these
stereotypes were not revised but, rather, perpetuated.
Hence all men were alternately tricky, exciting, and dangerously self-seeking or else they were devalued, disgusting,
or depressing. During analysis these stereotypes were
approximated to current self and object images, with appropriate and gradual revision. As a result of improved
recognition of real possibilities, she developed a more appropriate and extensive repertoire of potential roles. This
helped her to act differently, to understand people better,
and to obtain social reinforcement for her improvement.

The overstimulating oedipal father and the hostile,
withholding, "bad," pregenital mother were *both* perpetual
stereotypes for "role-casting" others *and* were warded off
from conscious and emotional experience. Nonrecognition
was necessary because both stereotypes led to relationships
in which she was exquisitely vulnerable to reactive anxiety
and guilt. The analytic situation allowed her first to test the
analyst by her various transference *behaviors*. When he was
neither excessively nice nor excessively mean, it became
safe to begin to *experience* the maternal transference; just as
when the analyst was neither too provocative nor too
remote or "selfish," she could begin to experience the
paternal transference. With transference experience came
childhood memories linked to the particular feeling state as
well as acting out of the configurations in extra analytic
current relationships. The combination of childhood memories, transference experience, and a certain amount of
"playing out" in real life led to greater freedom to express
childlike emotional expression and to alter the stereotyped

self-object schemata. She thus matured in that she surrendered both pregenital and oedipal demands upon the world, and at the same time shed the demands on her for fear and retribution. These changes will be reviewed in greater detail in the final section of this chapter when revision of schemata is discussed.

Structural and topographic points of view

In the structural point of view, one differentiates three sets of functions. One is ego or "I-like" functions; the second is id or "it-like" drives; the third is superego or functions of value and conscience-like appraisals of self from a vantage of morals, ideals, and social conventions. Topography refers to conscious, preconscious, and unconscious levels of information and information processing. Elements in the preconscious can be raised upon volition to consciousness, not so for unconscious elements.

Before analysis Miss Smith operated with constricted ego functions. The functions most severely affected were attention deployment, conscious thought, memory, and fantasy. Her experience of emotion was inhibited. She feared any strong feelings and reacted to them as if they were intrusive and uncontrollable forces. Overgeneralization of associations led her to her own reactions to her peers by the same standards she had used to treat her wishes toward her parents. Taboos against sexual and aggressive strivings were primitive and led to a strong predisposition towards guilt. Like the primary impulses, guilty feelings were repressed and yet occasionally made peremptory incursions into conscious awareness.

Because of the general use of repression and denial, she seldom knew exactly what she wished and could not plan effective action towards gratification. Instead, there was episodic emotional experience, especially of anxiety, without clear relationship of the feelings to ideational representations.

Conscious experience had to be avoided not only because of the guilty responses that might occur, but because thoughts were equated with actions. This posture was based on her own fears of loss of control and the Church position that thought could be sinful. These attitudes were reexamined during analysis, and she learned to qualify differences between thought and action. As thought could be experienced in terms of conflictual areas, she was able to review and rework the various attitudes that contributed to conflict.

This review process had many facets, not the least of which was the development of an integrated set of ego ideals. At the onset of analysis she had little sense of an authentic autonomous self. She preferred the "swinger" self representation to the depressed, neurotic, childlike self representation that seemed the only alternative. Either role was in conflict with values that were not integrated into the self schemata but functioned rather as introjects of mother and father. When she experienced herself as a sexually active swinger, she was vulnerable to internal experiences of an introject of her rule-bound, sin-preoccupied mother. This sense of another person reprimanding her was a form of self-criticism for being corrupt and evil. When she experienced herself as a good girl who worked responsibly to do her duty, then an equivalent introject, associated with her father, excoriated her for being a passive victim—dead, inhibited, uninteresting, and stupidly compliant. In either instance, the values seemed to have their own activity, separate from her self image.

In the course of the analysis, she realized the extent to which the various value systems were components of her self schemata. She could reexamine her standards and revise attitudes that she did not feel were rational or in accord with her growing sense of adult morality. As a way of regulating life choices, she began to adhere to a set of principles, actively avowed by the self, rather than to punishment-oriented fears.

At first, the acquisition of new cognitive skills and the modification of old cognitive habits occurred because of the positive relationship with the therapist. This relationship was based on both the therapeutic alliance, with its components of realistic hope and trust, and the positive transference with its component fantasies of love and attention. The strength of the introjected therapist, part real and part fantasy, counteracted the strength of parental introjects because he was the immediate potential source of rewards and punishments. The power of ideas attributed to the therapist, such as the acceptability of thinking the unthinkable, gained ascendancy over equivalent ideas about criticism attributed to parents and God. Later, as transference fantasies were relinquished, she tended to identify with the therapist's neutral, objective, rational, thoughtful, reality-attentive, patient, and nonjudgmental operations. Thus she learned to conceptualize clearly where she once had been globally vague. The learning occurred both by the trial and error discovery that clarity helped her to feel in control, and by the automatic learning that goes with valuation of and identification with another person.

Dynamic and economic points of view

The dynamic point of view deals with interacting forces, especially wishes, feared consequences of wishes, and defenses or controls of impulses to prevent such threats by warding off ideas and emotions. The economic point of view deals with the intensity of these forces in terms of types of motives.

As described in previous sections, two clusters of warded-off mental contents and typical defensive operations characterized her dynamics. One cluster was oedipal in configuration. The second was concerned with pregenital ambivalence centered on her mother.

In the oedipal cluster, sexual strivings towards her father conflicted with (1) taboos against incest, (2) fear of competitive maternal retaliation, and (3) fear of loss of control and sexual assault. Secondary themes in this cluster included destructive wishes against mother and father with reactive guilt. The destructive wishes against her father included a desire to wrest from him the penis and the power it symbolized. The destructive wishes against her mother included a desire to take adult female genitalia and child-bearing capacities away from her and to assume the mother's role in the family. Destructive wishes also concerned her sisters. If she could rid the family of them, she could occupy their positions.

This complex of preoedipal and oedipal themes was particularly difficult to work through during childhood because she was dealing not only with her own unconscious fantasy but also the added danger of her father's real sexual displays. If she were exhibitionistic herself or voyeuristically interested in him, then she might lose control. Her principal method of warding off these threats was inhibition of sensation, thought, and action. Total inhibition maintained emotional states within tolerable limits. But the relative strength of strivings and external stimulation exceeded her capacity for complete avoidance. Under threat of a partial failure in repressive maneuvers, she experienced intrusive attacks of anxiety and guilt which she saw as dangerous lapses of control, even if ideation remained unclear. To reduce the threat, secondary defenses such as displacement were instituted, resulting in the formation of symptoms such as phobias and hypochondriasis.

The change process involved revising the impulse-defense configuration for this cluster of themes. The first step was confrontation, so that she recognized the extensiveness of denial as a defensive maneuver. Awareness led to control and altered the balance of forces between defensive and impulsive aims. Conscious thought increased, and she found herself able to tolerate clarity.

For example, as she tested out the analyst in the transference situation, she found him safely nonreactive to her provocations. This sense of safety and attention to her tendency to deny emotionally what she was doing behavioristically led to awareness that she was acting out exhibitionistic and voyeuristic fantasies. These current behavioral strivings were then conceptualized. Once conceptualized, the ideas and feelings could be linked associatively with childhood memories, hitherto repressed in large part, of her felt emotions and response to her father's behavior. The segregation of memory fragments decreased, allowing a coherent story to emerge.

Once defensive maneuvers were less mandatory, there

was a general decrease in tension, and she could bend her capacities to other efforts. As memories and fantasies could be reviewed in conscious secondary-process thought, primary-process associations and appraisals became less powerful as determinants of responsivity to events. For example, she could get to know the qualities of a new male acquaintance by checking and rechecking her perceptions and appraisals, rather than by entering into a role relationship based on primitive stereotypes.

The second main cluster of warded-off contents was already labeled as pregenital. It included an unconscious evaluation of herself as insufficiently nurtured as a child and led to arousal of depression and rage. These emotions were averted by repression, denial, rationalization, fantasy distortion of reality, and reaction formation.

She could also use undoing, although not to the extent found in obsessional personalities. When anxiety and guilt, provoked by the first cluster of sexual themes, emerged in the analysis, she would shift the organization of her experience to the second cluster of deprivation themes. These deprivation themes evoked a mood state that oscillated between resigned helplessness and a kind of angry sadness, and tended to reduce sexual excitation.

THE PSYCHODYNAMIC-
COGNITIVE POINT OF VIEW

The foregoing statements were formulations from the six psychoanalytic metapsychological points of view. Modification of defensive operations is central to the changes asserted within each point of view and necessitated a redundancy in statements. The limitations of the foregoing statements lie in the absence of specification about the modification and revision of these defensive operations. The modification of defenses, as they occur in the form of resistances, is essential if a complete transference neurosis (or neuroses) is to evolve and be resolved. In the following section the focus is on the cognitive processes by which defenses are accomplished and the alterations of cognitive structure that may then take place. An emphasis on new learning will be added to the familiar concepts of insight, working through, and conflict resolution.

Patterns of Change in Ideas and Feelings

Miss Smith manifested many of the characteristics accorded the prototype of the hysterical personality. Shapiro (1965) has given the most authoritative and penetrating analysis of how these traits are mediated by particular cognitive styles. Along with other leading theorists of cognitive controls, Shapiro emphasizes the impressionistic distortions of incoming perceptual stimuli, the rapid and short-circuited appraisal of meanings, and the limited categories and availability of memory as central aspects of thought in the hysterical person (Gardner et al. 1959, Klein et al. 1962).

For the description of shifts in the neurotic cognitive style of Miss Smith, it is desirable to describe clearly segments of the cognitive process, from perception to decisive completion of a train of thought. Then the change in each segment can be discussed in terms of the treatment

process and final outcome. To prevent excessive segmenta-
lization, four areas for discussion have been selected and
will be labeled as perceptual attention, representation,
association, and resolution of incongruities.

Perceptual Attention

Miss Smith habitually deployed her attention in a global
manner. Her descriptions of events were vague and impressionistic and left the listener with little sense of the context
or order of events. It is possible that this trait might have
been a style of communication, but as the analyst empa-
thized and entered deeply into the patient's experience, it
seemed that the vagueness extended to her perceptions as
well and was not simply an inhibited form of speech. She
described events that occurred within the analytic hour in
the same way; and when asked about the quality of her
experience, she confirmed these inferences.

At the same time, details of the environment (such as
oral and sexual symbols) that might relate to her current
wishful and fearful expectancies were hyperattended. This
is a general characteristic of object-seeking, attention, and
thought organization in a hysterical personality (Fairbairn
1954, Myerson 1969, Wisdom 1961). That is, details of the
environment symbolically relevant to such concerns were
discovered rapidly, but not accurately appraised.

While she was quick to note the surface attitudes of
another person, she seemed unaware of her own acts, of
what was revealed by her facial expression or bodily gestures. She might move her head coquettishly or swing her
legs and not realize that she was doing this.

Such imprecision of perception seemed to be due to a too-rapid construction of images, an overreadiness for con-clusion, and an overusage of expectancy schemata. Percep-tual rechecking, which would have counteracted a rapid illusion such as seeing a man on the street and thinking he was the analyst, was seldom utilized, so that errors of assumption and extended illusions occurred.

During analysis the defensive reasons for not recog-nizing her own actions were interpreted. Paradoxically, her vagueness of perception was called to her attention. These interventions (as effected by the nature of the immediate transference situation) led her to conscious efforts at coun-teracting her automatic, nonconscious tendencies in areas of perception and attention. She slowly learned to notice details, observe her own acts, and gather clues about her own motivational states and those of others. This learning was made possible by her increased tolerance for emotional responses to the incoming information. Increased aware-ness led to all the other changes in information processing just as, transactively, the changes in how she processed information produced a wider repertoire of expectancy schemata and increased perception.

Representation

Information can gain expression in lexical, image (in var-ious sensory systems), and enactive (bodily) modes of rep-resentation (Horowitz 1972, 1988). Any person's style can be discussed in terms of his habitual usage of and transla-tions between the three styles. In an "ideal" person, repre-sentation in one mode could be readily translated into other forms of representation. Such cross-modal expression gives breadth and depth to meaning. Miss Smith habitually used enactive and image modes for conflicted mental contents and tended to inhibit translation of such information into words.

Her enactive representations included body movements indicative of sexual interest. As mentioned in the previous section, her awareness of these expressions was quite limited. She neither saw herself behaving provocatively, nor labeled a posture, gesture, or facial expression with such specific words.

Representations of images derived through perception were also affected by a particular style. As already indicated, schemata of expectancy had relative dominion. These expectations could force a perceptual sampling of external reality into a template configured by what Knapp (1974) would call her long-standing interpersonal fantasies. The dynamic themes of looking and being seen, sexual interest, guilt, anxiety, and anger provided many such templates. The results were representations that composited sets of information from within and without, but were heavily slanted towards the internal contributants.

These contributants to a given representation were scrutinized carefully in multiple episodes of microanalysis of a conflictual experience (Horowitz 1974). The verbal nature of the analytic situation, the prevailing demand for translation of experience into words, led to reports of details beyond her personal tendency for vague and global descriptions. If she were describing an emotionally difficult event, such as an encounter with a potential male friend, fragments of representation of what happened would gradually be pieced together. Reconstructive efforts fleshed out the context of the episode and sequence of interactions. Reconstructions could be contrasted with her initially vague and perhaps distorted image representations of what had happened. Similar processes clarified the patient-analyst situation. These recurrent efforts led to changes in her ability to experience immediate situations. In addition to experiencing the interrelationships of meanings expressed in enactive and image modes, she was able to verbalize what was happening.

Free association, for Miss Smith, meant a preponderance of visual images which, for communication to the analyst, she then translated into words. Often this translation was blocked; she trailed off, said, "I don't know," and became silent in mid-phrase. The pressure of the analyst's presence, in and of itself, motivated her to work towards more fluid translation of these images. Fantasy images, in general, tended to dominate her conscious experience.

The images of the fantasies were generally disguised wish-fulfilments. Since her wishes involved object relationships, in contrast to the self-aggrandizing role fantasies of more narcissistic patients, two people might be depicted in the image representations. Remarkably, neither person might be designated as "self." If she imagined a particular man she had seen as flirting with a woman, it might be unclear whether she was the woman or whether she imagined watching another woman. Conceptualization could be even more vague. The idea of someone losing control and hurting someone else could be visualized without any particular awareness of whether she were the person losing control or being injured. Once again, the pressure of the analytic situation contributed to motivation to label the images as self and others. Early in treatment the demand was simply for reports. Later the analyst interpreted images in terms of what she wished or feared from others. Finally she continued to elaborate images, including translation to lexical associative meanings, until the self references became clear. Of course, interpretations of fear of activity and of defensive switches between activity and passivity played an important role. The central point is that the increased translation of images and enactions into words was due not only to modification of defenses and estimation of danger but was also a process of acquired skill.

While lexical representation was not excluded from her experience of thought, there was a virtual absence of some types of verbal naming. She neither spoke nor let herself think the words for genitals or bodily functions. Penis, vagina, nipple, bladder, urine, and feces were referred to as "it." She could not imagine herself as ever being able to think clearly, much less speak, in such terms. This issue of lexical vagueness was then elaborated into transference attitudes. She expected the analyst to try to force her to say sexual words, and anticipated her own resistance and the excitement of the chase.

These transference meanings were worked through, along with recognition of the general defensive function of lexical avoidances. Use of the lexical system meant a fuller orchestration of thought and a sharper designation of her own role, since in grammatical construction the subject and object are usually specified: "I want him to do it to me." The image system may clarify what "it" is; the enactive system may clarify the intensity of doing it; the verbal system states the cause and effect sequence. Enhanced verbal communication led her to specify what she felt and wanted. At the end of the analysis she felt especially pleased

with her acquired ability to speak frankly, clearly, and to
the point, in various contexts. She eventually advanced her
career by taking on public speaking engagements.

To summarize, automatic inhibitions changed during
analysis as the deployment of attention was altered. Interventions by the analyst directed her attention to the possibility of representation. Conscious efforts, motivated by
both alliance and by transference attitudes modified the
automatic nonconscious inhibitory operations. As representation occurred, the situation proved safer than expected. Recurrent safety where, originally, danger had been
signaled, modified her automatic appraisal of threat and
arousal of anxiety. Repetition of conscious efforts at representation altered the "programming" of thought until representation and translation became the automatic formats.

Intrusive representations, often as images, were commonplace before and during the early phases of analysis. A
loss of volitional control was an aspect of this experience
because the expressions occurred in spite of inhibitory
efforts. These episodes were themselves interpreted as
events and indicated to her that she was out of control. She
feared that such experiences meant insanity, yet the idea
had some appeal. The secondary gain would be the opportunity to use madness to force those who neglected her to
care for her.

In the course of conscious efforts at representation of
usually inhibited ideas, she gained the sense of herself as
active thinker of all thoughts. She tolerated threatening
ideas and the resulting emotions. Because active thought
was permitted, intrusive episodes lessened. While this process deserves further explication, the result of the increased

conscious effort at representation was a sense of increased control.

Associational Linkages, Networks, and the Appraisal of Information

One can postulate that any potentially new event sets in motion a series of appraisal problems as a kind of program for thought processes (Lazarus 1966, Klein 1967, Peterfreund 1971). The program would continue as a conceptual tendency until the ability to fit a new event into relevant cognitive structures or schemata was exercised (Piaget 1937, Jacobson 1954, Thompkins 1962, Miller, Galanter, and Pribram 1960). Reinterpretation of new events or revision of schemata would fit new to old and so complete the process. Until such completion, codings of the event and relevant associations would tend towards recurrent representation. These representations would be experienced as intrusive if the repetition tendency were opposed by inhibitory maneuvers (Horowitz 1970, 1986, Horowitz and Becker 1972).

At the onset of analysis Miss Smith was guided by the pleasure-unpleasure principle. The reality principle also regulated cognition, but not to the extent ideal for adaptation. For example, in establishing the relationship of a new event to enduring schematic classifications, she tended to short-circuit, i.e., to erroneously "recognize" the new information as if it were another instance of a long-standing interpersonal fantasy.

Ever expecting a rescuer, she appraised a chance encounter with a man as if he were the rescuer and "this was
it." Associations to available memories of times when similar feelings led to disappointment were inhibited because
the need for rescue was great and the idea of not being
rescued was intolerable. This type of inhibition of associational possibilities was accomplished by terminating and
not translating the first glimmerings of representations that
threatened to arouse negative affect.

In order to move away from threatening ideas, she
would declare a train of thought completed or incapable of
completion. These styles were reflected in her speech.
Either she declared, "I do not know," or she prematurely
closed a topic by announcing she knew the meanings. "I do
not know," the virtual hallmark of communication of the
hysterical character, was not only a statement of fact but
also an injunction against further thought—an injunction
now internalized but once a family style.

The repeated avoidance of possible and relevant associational routes led to a low capacity for organizing and
analyzing events in terms of cause and effect sequences. She
was unable to predict her own actions or plan for interpersonal situations. To the extent that she recognized this
impairment she suffered narcissistic injuries and also feared
being out of control or overwhelmed by decisiveness in
others. Such fear further motivated inhibitions of thought
because thinking might involve knowing her bad thoughts,
knowledge would lead to peremptory action, and loss of
control and powerlessness over intrusive fantasies would
follow.

Because of her fears of being bad or out of control, she
automatically suppressed associational lines about her own

activity. If ideas were evolving that designated her as active and if anxiety and guilt increased with such ideas, she shifted associational lines to those that designated her as passive. Sometimes inhibition and shifting were insufficient and anxiety and guilt mounted. Another operation to reduce these felt emotions was to lose her reflective self-awareness, a part of a dissociative process. In such altered states of consciousness, she could not remember what she had just been thinking or perceiving.

For example, after deciding to lose her virginity and learn about sex, she entered impulsively into an affair. She could not, however, do so while conceptualizing herself as awake and aware. She had to be seduced while drunk. Later, while she knew that intercourse had taken place, she was unsure of what it had been like. In plaintive and poignant terms during the analysis she described herself as psychologically a virgin because she had never actively and freely engaged in sex in a tender union.

Altered states of consciousness had the additional advantages of changing the type of mental contents she experienced. Instead of genitally-tinged wishes and fears, she fantasied a kind of oceanic nurturing. The distinction between reality and fantasy was blurred, making reality less disappointing and fantasy more enjoyable. Disparate attitudes could be dissociated with ease.

To recapitulate, there are a series of cognitive options available when the person with a hysterical personality wishes to repress. The options of how to deal with ideas that might activate painful emotional states are:

1. Inhibit representation of the ideas and feelings.
2. If option 1 fails, then inhibit translation of those ideas

into other modes of representation (e.g., don't let images translate into word labels).

3. Avoid associational connections (i.e., use steps 1 and 2 to avoid ideas and feelings that are automatically elicited by information that has gained representation).

4. Conclude a train of thought by early closure or declaration of impossibility of solution.

5. Change self attitude from active to passive, or vice versa, depending on the direction of greater threat.

6. If above measures are inadequate, alter state of consciousness.

Each of these cognitive maneuvers could be recognized as experiences. Miss Smith was, of course, unaware that these were her cognitive habits when she began analysis. But each operation could be explicitly interpreted in the context of some specific mental content and emotional response. With direction of attention to the flow of cognitive experience, she could become aware of what she was doing and try to do otherwise. A train of thought prematurely closed off could be resumed and further associations elaborated.

If she were alone, she would not behave this way. With the analyst she felt both safe enough and pressured enough to counteract her automatic avoidance. The pressure came from the therapeutic alliance, since she rightly believed that she and the therapist shared a value placed on full representation and communication (Greenson 1965), and from the transference relationship. She expected the therapist to be pleased and attentive if she cooperated with his wishes.

Whatever the weight of multiple motives, her conscious efforts to represent, to know, and to speak the previously unthinkable had a gradual effect. The warded-off complexes of ideas and feelings were found to be tolerable to her adult mind, although they had been appraised as intolerable by her childhood mind. Avoidance was less necessary. She worked through warded-off complexes and also learned a new way of thinking by repeated trials of representation and of cross-translation of image, enactive, and lexical representation.

Only partial changes in cognitive style occurred at any one time. Every major theme surfaced again and again, each time with additional nuances and greater clarity. During episodes of positive transference she could accept with complete understanding her erotic yearnings, her anxieties and guilt feelings, her inclinations not to know, and the relevant associational networks. With each repetition there was less resistance, less interpretation necessary, and greater definition of herself as active.

The above statements applied to periods of working through in which Miss Smith responded to an interpretation with introspective efforts. There were many times when she experienced an interpretive activity of the analyst, even simple repetitions of her own phrases, as if the analyst were teasing or exciting her. She was being forced to attend to the weird ideas of the analyst, just as her father forced his nudity upon her. Such transference projections clouded the clarity of the immediate topic but added the immediate emotionality so essential to therapeutic change.

Clarity about the transference was then necessary. The modifications of self and object schemata through transference and transference interpretation will be discussed more thoroughly in the following section, but the point to be made here is that no cognitive change could occur without work on the transference. The reduction in repressive maneuvers required a combination of cognitive interpretations, cognitive learning, working through of warded-off ideas and feelings, and alteration of patterns of self and object relationships.

As inhibitory operations became less automatic and peremptory, Miss Smith found she could maintain conceptual time and space on a given topic. She developed increased confidence in her ability to confront conflictual topics without "runaway" emotions or thoughts. Once she could stop thinking about a given topic because she could control her thinking, she could let herself explore it more. As Weiss (1967) has pointed out, the conscious control ability of deliberate suppression made the unconscious defensive use of repression less necessary. As ideational-emotional complexes were worked through, conflict was reduced and there was far less tension between emergent ideas and inhibitory operations. Correspondingly, intrusive episodes occurred less frequently, her feeling of being in control was affirmed by experience, and her self-confidence allowed her to take increased risks in behavior.

Resolving Incongruities

Association and appraisal do not complete cognitive processing. A newly represented set of information, whether from an external event or from emergent dreams, fantasies, or memories, may not fit existing schemata about the self, objects, or the world. Cognitive processing would be complete only when the discrepancy between the new concepts and the enduring attitudes was reduced. Either the new concept must be revised or the enduring attitudes changed. Miss Smith had a conspicuous tendency to appraise new information so that it would fit her enduring schemata when, realistically, her schemata were inappropriate and should have been modified. Failure to change these enduring schemata led to a shallow repertoire of human knowledge (Shapiro 1965).

She behaved inappropriately, and these actions led, sometimes, to startling confrontations. Suddenly people no longer fit her mental model of them. And if they were not as she believed, then she was not as she believed. She felt either betrayed or depersonalized. Such depersonalization experiences were sufficient triggers for anxiety attacks or shifts to alternate self schemata. For example, if she were behaving with a man in the role of glamorous swinger and the man laughed at some trifling lack of poise, she might suddenly and globally change into a clumsy, depressed, waiflike person. Alternately, she might be unable to control a display of emotions such as panic, weeping, or rage. These inappropriate reactions interfered with relationships and further demolished her sense of confidence.

During analysis she learned to review the fit between object expectations and object representations. Once she could think more clearly, she could recheck the ideational route that led her to form an internal model of a given person and relationship. These cognitive processes made it possible to revise her self and object schemata. From a limited repertoire that resulted in global roles, she was able to move to particular traits, thus fleshing out her internal models of the world and increasing the range of possibilities for active plans.

Cognitive Process and Cognitive Structure

Cognitive change allows the transference situation, past memories, and current patterns of interpersonal relationship to be examined and reappraised by using the tools of conscious thought. The transference neurosis itself would not develop fully without the analytic situation and the process of interpreting resistances. As Weiss (1967, 1971) has pointed out, the manifestations of transference themselves may not occur until the analyst and the analytic situation have passed behavioral tests safely. For example, if the analyst were too kind to Miss Smith and yielded to her demands for extra care, then the pregenitally based hostility within the maternal transference might never have been analyzed (Wallerstein 1986). This sequence, from warding off transferences based on primitive schemata to revision of schemata in the direction of maturity can be shown diagrammatically as in Figure 9-1. In essence, the stages are (1) warding off, (2) transference tests (e.g., asking for special times for appointments), (3) transference emergence, and then—*granted changes in cognitive style*—(4) recognition of what it *feels* like is happening as appraised in relation to what is *really* happening. This latter step leads to revision of primitive schemata of the self and others and relates to Loewald's (1960) view that transference interpretations have two elements; they take the patient to their

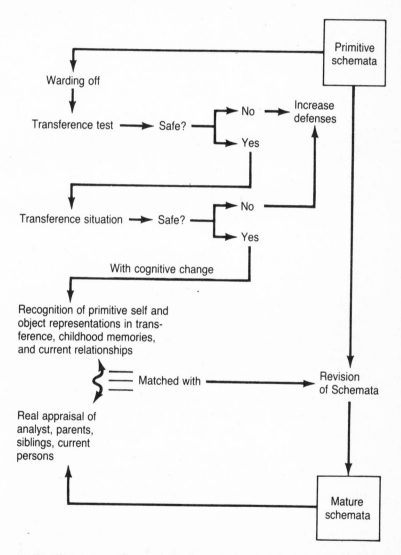

FIGURE 9-1 Change in Schemata during Psychoanalysis

true regressive level, and they also indicate to the patient the higher integrative level to be reached.

SELF AND OBJECT
SCHEMATA

The oedipal and preoedipal oral situation provided the core meanings of Miss Smith's self and object schemata, as in many instances of hysterical character (Marmor 1953, Easser and Lesser 1965, Zetzel 1970). The main configuration was a positive attachment to her father with an ambivalent and identifying relationship to her mother. She also had positive longings for her mother. While primarily one of oral striving, this theme had been partially sexualized into homosexual ideas. This negative oedipal configuration was also used as a defense against the positive version. Another important aspect of the negative oedipal configuration was identification with her father, especially with his aesthetic interests and capabilities.

The two sisters must be added to form a map of the conflictual family patterns. The result is shown in Figure 9-2. Note that each person is given a title according to his or her predominant role in the family. Father was the "special exception," older sister the "free spirit," and so on. An arrow from Miss Smith to each person and the main bonds between other persons indicates her primary negative feelings. Anxiety and guilt are omitted because they are reactions to the attitudes shown.

From these classical oedipal configurations and sibling rivalries, one can abstract Miss Smith's main role schemata. Of the main constructs for childhood differentiation of

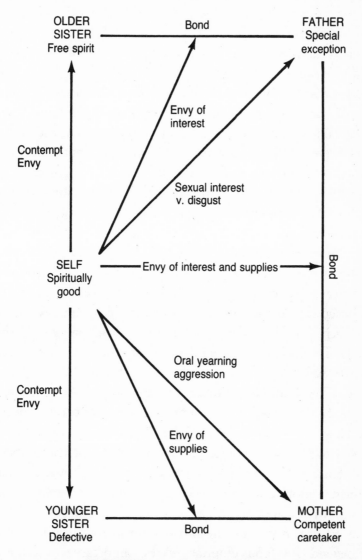

FIGURE 9-2 Family Schemata

persons, three were the most important for her (see Kelly 1955, Loevinger 1973). They were gender, goodness, and degree of relative activity. The three dichotomous constructs form eight possible combinations (good, male, and active; good, female, and active, etc.). The main traits, roles, and schemata created by combination of constructs, can be tabulated in terms of her four closest relatives and herself (see Table 9-1). This contrivance catalogs the split-apart schemata of her ambivalently held family members.

The problem for analysis was to identify these primitive roles, including precursors of more differentiated roles, and to help them evolve into forms more congruous with the real potentials for interpersonal relationships in her adult life, independent of her family.

This analytic task was complicated by her ability and tendency to take either role in a two-person dyad. As emphasized earlier, she could interchange active and passive roles in her inner experience of any given stimulation. She could be the moralist condemning a sexually active "swinger," or the swinger, living more pleasurably than the moralist and at a higher level than the defective child-woman.

This fluid ability to change the set for self in a given role-dyad is based on childhood development. Baldwin (as reviewed by Loevinger 1973) called this the dialectic of personal growth: The child learns to perceive the traits of parents, then can find such patterns in the self, which then permits more differentiated perception of the parents, and so on in a reciprocal process. As a result, almost everything found in the self is something found in significant others. Loewald (1960) has emphasized the importance of resumption of such developmental process in understanding the therapeutic action of the transference and real object relationship in psychoanalysis.

Miss Smith's parents and sisters were models for her self development as well as mirrors that reflected the development of her self concept. The defectiveness of her parents as models and mirrors interfered with her maturation, and the analytic process allowed both a resumption of construct development and an opportunity to resolve conflicts between constructs.

Revision of Object Schemata

Before analysis, her object schemata—what Knapp (1974) has called "interpersonal fantasy constellations"—were polarized into good and bad versions of main figures. Her father, for example, was separably conceived of as an idealized rescuer and as the bad father who embodied failure and perversity. While these schemata seldom became conscious, they organized her interpretations of current interpersonal contexts and hence her interpersonal patterns.

Cognitive processing, as described in the previous section, allowed active schemata to be reviewed. The transference allowed here and now reenactments that could be compared with the realities of the therapeutic process and relationship. Any particular schemata was labeled, known by many facets, connected with current extra-analytic relationships and with recollections of childhood.

Such reviews meant a new integration of segregated constructs. By the end of the analysis she could view her parents as real people, with both good and bad traits. Clarity in perception of these patterns engendered revision

TABLE 9.1. Role Structure

Main constructs			Roles of others				Self roles
Goodness	Activity	Gender	Mother	Father	Older sister	Younger sister	
Good	Active	Female	Competent, child-bearing, caring, moralistic		Sensuous, free, child-bearing		Sexually active, "swinger," moralistic
Good	Passive	Female				Deserving attention	Sick and deserving child
Bad	Active	Female	Manipulator, devouring		Promiscuous, sinful		Incestuous, devouring, rivalrous
Bad	Passive	Female	Depressed, depleted woman			Defective child	Defective child-woman

Good	Active	Male	Skillful	Grandiose fantasies of being skillful, effective
Good	Passive	Male	Aesthetic, soulful	Aesthetic, soulful artist
Bad	Active	Male	Sexually intrusive, out-of-control	Out-of-control person
Bad	Passive	Male	Failure	Incompetent, failure

of her memory of the past and of her future expectations. She gave up the hope of finding her parents transformed into ideals, developed a sympathetic understanding of their failures, and relinquished the belief that they were deliberately causing her suffering.

This increased clarity about schemata derived from relationships with her family allowed her to control her development of schemata of new people. Aware of her tendencies to externalize and project, she could check supposed similarities to see if they were borne out by real behavior. With new ways to act, her relationships became increasingly fresh and real.

Modifications of Self Schemata

The various constructs of Table 9-1 clustered into four main forms of self experience. The most frequent was the organization of information about herself as if she were passive, defective, and childlike. The second most frequent self experience was of her idealized self. The components of this ideal were not fully integrated and consisted in the role of the sexually free spirit and that of the artistic and soulful. Unfortunately, these ideal self experiences were unstable. They changed readily into the passive defective self, as indicated by the heavy arrow in Figure 9-3, or in the direction of bad activity, becoming the incestuous, devouring, manipulative, and out-of-control self experience. This third state was usually warded off, but surfaced at times as an involuntary experience.

The fourth kind of self experience was as a moralist. In

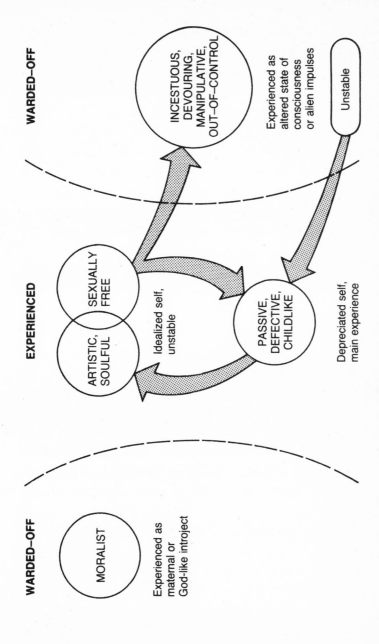

FIGURE 9-3 Varieties of Self Experience

the moral schemata, accusations were directed against past or anticipated acts of the self or others. This state was also warded off and might also intrude. The intrusive episodes were conscious experiences of felt presences in the form of maternal or God-like introjects. These four types of self experience are sufficient to pattern her self schemata at the onset of analysis; it remains to describe how they changed.

As with object schemata, changes in self schemata relied upon concurrent changes in cognitive operations. Reduced inhibitory controls allowed conscious comparisons between the current real facts and her enduring schemata. Discrepancies between schemata and real behaviors were recognized. Instead of revising the "here and now" information to fit her stereotypes, she was able in the analysis to change the schemata.

Changes in the Sexually Free Self Schemata

Before analysis, the main manifestation of the sexually free schemata was her role of "swinger." Frequent sexual liaisons revolved around victim and aggressor roles. She was one or the other; her partner occupied the complementary role. In the swinger role, unable to conceptualize two simultaneously active persons, she invariably gave one a passive script. The aggressor takes from or seduces the victim. The victim gives up or submits. Sometimes the roles are reversed with sadomasochistic flavorings.

The swinger role was an adaptational attempt to defy self images as the victim of her mother's insufficient attentiveness and her father's seductions. While she imagined herself as if she were the aggressor, luring and breaking the hearts of men and arousing the envious fury of women, she also submitted to sexual usage and was ultimately discarded. Only with older or "greyer" men or during the vain attempts of virile men to lead her to sexual climax, could she feel as if she actively defeated them.

The possibilities of both persons being active, as is desirable in sexual transactions, or of both persons being passive, as in quiet mutuality, were too anxiety-provoking. If both persons were active, this meant exciting each other and revived a prototypical oedipal danger that she and her father would be interested in each other simultaneously. It was only during analysis that she could learn to contemplate dual activity. For example, later in the analysis, she felt correctly that she and the analyst were working intensively together, attempting to understand the multiple meanings of an episode of experience. At such times she would have a "reality" experience; she would be amazed at the active cooperation, feel dizzy, and fear that she would wet or stain the couch from a sudden loss of sphincter control. She was so sure of the possibility that on occasion she checked the back of her skirt for stains before leaving the office.

Before she learned this new schemata, which involved activity on the part of both persons, she had to interpret the analytic situation as one of victim and aggressor. Either the analyst was forcing interpretations upon her, or she was the aggressor, overwhelming and draining the drab and tired analyst. The instability of the idealized state of being a sexually free person led to episodes of humiliation. When she saw another attractive female patient leave or enter, she fantasied that this was the exciting mistress of a famous politician or the analyst's wife, and felt rejected and defective.

As cognitive inhibitions were reduced, every aspect of these changes in experience could be worked out. The basic schemata were recurrently confronted. As already described, she used fantasy and projective identification to form new models. She softened the stereotype of "swinger" into a womanly, tender, sensuous set of traits. She daydreamed and dreamed of mutually active relationships in an idealized projection of the analyst and his wife. After these fantasy trials proved safe, she gradually experimented in reality. The inevitable disappointments did not deter her, because she could now tolerate and work them through consciously. Instead of imitating her ideal role models globally, she was now able to act out discretely some idealized traits. She was no longer an actress faking a part and ready for the humiliating experience of being unmasked.

The idealized self image also contains aesthetic and soulful qualities. These traits were not fully integrated with the concept of sexual freedom and sensuality. Because sexuality was dangerous, it was isolated from other ideals. Even the aesthetic and soulful ideals, however, were unstable. She was unable to work either on artistic or career oriented tasks, and so her self image could not be compared with these ideals without deflation. Since she could not bolster her self-esteem with memory or anticipation of real accomplishments, she could only daydream. Even that seemed, at times, so hopeless as to lead to depression and a shift to a self-as-defective position.

In the course of the analysis, ideals were confronted. She could decide again, as an adult now, which ideal she preferred. She could equilibrate goals to realistic appraisals of possibilities, thus changing adolescent grandiose fantasies into achievable expectations. She was able to dissociate artistic enterprises from her father's behavior. For example, she reviewed memories in which her father had given her a set of oil paints, a bottle of turpentine, and some canvas boards, and expected her to teach herself to paint landscapes and portraits. She had tried and performed only at a mediocre and frustrating level. Since she shared her father's ideas that she ought to learn by osmosis or spontaneous talent, she had explained this failure as her own incompetence.

Clear review of these ideas allowed her to reevaluate the memories. As an adult, she knew that training and practice were necessary to any skill. She then planned to take courses in technique. In executing this plan, she developed an interest in color mixing and perspective and found the step-by-step learning to be exhilarating.

These real and gratifying accomplishments provided the necessary memories for a stable idealized self image, and she was able to separate ideas of her own artistic interests and qualities from those ideas about her father and those ideas her father had about her. Then she was able to praise or to criticize her own work and to do so from a semirealistic basis. She could admit failure in a given effort without feeling worthless.

Changes in the Moralistic Self Schemata

At the onset of analysis, Miss Smith was unaware that she felt guilty about her activity in general and her sexuality in particular. Her conscious thoughts dwelt on the desirability of sexual freedom. As she became aware of feeling bad about active wishes, she was depressed to find her own feelings of guilt. It seemed primitive to her and like a submission to the weird analytic ideas she expected to have forced upon her. But the ideas soon became clear and tolerable.

As memories and fantasies of the past were reexamined and linked to the present, she learned to dissociate sexual and aggressive aims from intrafamilial and hence taboo objects. Her rational thought countered the laws proclaimed in her childhood and the conditioned association that overgeneralized them. She became the instigator of rules of behavior.

At first this process seemed artificial and also time-consuming. Faced with a given decision point, she had to think through many ramifications in order to deviate from her automatically imposed inhibitions and disavowals of inhibitions. But, with repetition of decisions she developed new guiding principles, which illuminated new ways to arrive at automatic decisions. These guiding principles and automatic responses were then seen as self-determined feelings rather than punitive restrictions from external sources.

With these changes there was less discrepancy between sexual self-images and the once warded-off and now modified moralistic self. Attributes from both schemata could be represented consciously and simultaneously without guilt or anxiety. This increased the stability of the ideal self schemata and also made it unnecessary to ward off the residual aspects of the moralistic self schemata. There was thus a gradual coalescence of these two schemata and the two others still to be discussed.

Changes in the Schemata of Self
as Passive, Defective Child

As mentioned earlier, she typified role relationships as those between active and passive persons. The main version was herself in the passive, defective, waiflike role in a rescue fantasy. In a good outcome, because of her suffering, she would be found by an idealized parental figure, given the necessary ingredients (such as gradual sexual instruction), and then would become a whole person. The bad outcome was to be subjected to abuse by a malicious or sadistic person and to obtain thereby some small attention, to accumulate pain that would be traded in later for gratification by destiny and that would relieve the guilt accumulated from various oedipal fantasies. Since this fantasy was not allowed clear conscious representation, it only organized the processing of the information of her everyday life but was not revised according to events and appraisal of realistic probabilities. She remained a passive victim, to be duped or rescued by active others.

To paraphrase the question about dual activity in role structures, why couldn't two persons be thought of as being together but "passive" in their relationship? She could not conceive of persons at rest with one another because her needs were experienced as too intense and peremptory. She also felt defective and unworthy of attention. She was incapable of relating and incompetent at work. To feel like that and be with another person who was not actively engaging her meant only that she had to feel alone, empty, and neglected.

The treatment situation was ready-made to fit into her rescue fantasy, as exemplified by the dream of being taken to the home-sanatorium of the analyst. As she began to reveal herself and to feel that she was understood, the fantasy of waif and rescuer took over and organized her beliefs about what would happen next. The analyst would recognize her needs and fill the void in a moment of lyrical union. She expected things that did not happen, and in the vacuum of frustration her wishes emerged as conscious desires. Because of the cognitive shifts, she could appraise them as deviant from the therapeutic contract but could also understand their import as recurring patterns.

Provided that the opportunity for conceptual clarity was also present, the transference situation allowed repeated confrontation with such everyday frustrations. Every weekend and vacation there was a separation. Unexpected separations occurred with illnesses. She could, for example, see how much she wanted the analyst to take her home, how frequently she accepted intercourse with others out of a desire to be held, how frustrated she felt when recalling childhood memories. These real experiences evoked sadness, but the sadness was related to specific instances rather than a global self-assessment. It was tolerable to feel sad when lonely on a given night, if she did not have to go from there to endless feelings of hopelessness and despair.

As she gave up the fantasy of rescue, it was necessary to fulfil the expected functions herself. Again, cognitive processing allowed both exploration of hitherto warded-off associational connections and consideration of new and possible solutions to her motivational dilemmas. Dreams often preceded the explorations of themes in the analytic hours and may have been dreamed for the purpose of furthering the analytic process. For example, she had the intense desire to be taken to restaurants by men and expected this to take place after intercourse as if, in effect, she had paid in advance. As the role schemata shifted in analysis, she began to dream of going to restaurants alone. At first the dreams ended in anxiety. After the dreams seemed satisfactory, she attempted to act them out in real life. She had always been phobic of eating out alone. Her first step was to take food home from a hamburger stand, then to eat lunch at a busy counter-service place, and finally to eat dinner in a good restaurant. She felt uncomfortable but successful after this series. Once she felt capable of being active on her own, she then felt entitled to be more assertive of her desires when dating men.

Part of this reality appraisal was also helpful in allowing her to recognize the improbability of realizing her rescue fantasy. At best, only children are rescued and cared for as children. In her relationships with older men she could be babied, but at an expense she no longer cared to pay. If being a sick child did not lead to rescue, secondary gains were no longer present. The revision of the schemata toward more adult appraisals of herself was thus encouraged by the reduction in expectation of reward.

As the swinger schemata lost its utility and necessity as a disavowal of her sense of feminine inadequacy, it was possible to explore consciously her defective body image. She was surprised to realize, when she allowed herself to imagine her own genitals, that she could not visualize herself as having a vagina and other organs. In a way, not have a speakable word like "vagina" helped preserve her childlike status.

During intercourse she did not "know" her vagina. Temporarily, as she first became more distinctly aware, the experience changed. She then was afraid she would extend her body too far; she wanted to control and take away the penis, or even wrestle with and control all of the male body. These explorations in reality and fantasy led to an evolving sense of body image and bodily competence.

The ideas also involved other supposedly "masculine" attributes. She became strongly contemptuous of men who did not shift the gears of cars with verve. She bought her own sports car and enjoyed mastery of the stick shift. She imagined herself outgunning the analyst in car races.

The projective identification with the analyst's wife also allowed her to elaborate possible self-images in fantasy. She watched "Titsy" be sexy, maternal, and humane all at the same time and then tried to act that way herself. Again, the trials of conscious fantasy and acting according to new ideals seemed artificial at first, but with practice and confidence seemed natural.

As her experience range widened, she could become aware of attitudes related to her defective body image. She feared injury by an uncontrolled penis because of her erroneous belief in a tiny or nonexistent vagina. Her pronounced scopophilia was seen not only as a libidinal impulse and a defensive reversal of exhibitionism, but also as an intense desire to gain information about what bodies were like. Recognition of her own interest led to examination and reduction of moralistic prohibitions and to exploration of her body with mirrors and her fingers. She read books on sex and experimented in erotic stimulation. Each new experience led to anxiety, but in tolerable dosages. She realized her fear of "letting go" or becoming wildly aggressive. The fear could be matched with reality. It did not happen and the fearful expectation was revised. As her body image evolved, she felt sexually competent. She could let her alert anxiety during intercourse wane, and accumulate plateaus of erotic arousal.

Incestuous, Devouring, Out-of-Control Self

This final set of self attributes was warded off and experienced as intrusive, as was the moralistic self which opposed it.

At the onset of analysis Miss Smith was not aware of a self experience as an incestuous, devouring, and dangerously out-of-control child. Yet the potential of such states exerted dynamic effects. Rigid controls over self experience were fostered to avoid this state. It was, for example, better in a defensive sense to be the defective child at such times as the swinger image was not idealized but rather was associated with familial, oedipal meanings.

The rigid inhibitions gave way and recurrent father and mother transference episodes emerged. She experienced sexual wishes toward the analyst and also devouring aims, as if the ideational and affective emergence would be tantamount to action. The rule in the analytic situation of verbalizing rather than touching, and the consistent neutrality of the analyst in terms of the desires he might bring into the situation made for a safer experience of such thoughts and feelings than had been possible previously. Even her feelings of rivalry toward her sisters were given a foil in the analytic situation as she envied other patients more interesting or more needy than herself and as she evolved various feelings for her image of the analyst's presumed wife.

As the incestuous, devouring, rivalrous feelings emerged in self–object dyads, it was possible for her to realize that she originated these feelings, rather than that they were imposed upon her. As with the other roles, this out-of-control-self feeling could be compared with actual experiences. She did not break the analytic rule against physical confrontations, did not injure the analyst or blow up his car, did not tear into the walls or stain the couch. She only fantasized that she or other patients might do this. The distance between fantasy and reality grew. Fantasy became self-generated and controlled. Thus the conscious experience in the present was quite different from conscious experiences in childhood.

As she learned to experience strivings for erotic and tender attentions, she was able to contemplate further plans for obtaining gratifications. Just as the reduction in anxiety and guilt responses reduced the threat, anticipation of realistic possibilities made the experience of need less painful. She came to view the analyst as a trial object. She could experiment with various ways to contemplate herself and him. Then she could have a set of ideas, plans, and responses already partially worked out when she tried to allow herself such an open range of experience with other persons, persons who would respond to her according to their own wishes.

This course of trial-self feelings reduced the incestuous quality of her erotic interests. As the connections were made through associative extensions, she was able to change the object of her erotic-self feelings. The analyst provided a safe, early displacement. Then she could allow herself to experience excitement while with her male friends. She could learn to assert her sexuality without guilt or anxiety because she was able to perceive that the relationship was mutually satisfactory, that the associations to taboo or destructive components were inappropriate and could be deemphasized.

CONCLUSION

A case of hysterical personality was presented in terms of the history before and during analysis. The analytic outcome was good; the problem was the formulation of changes in patterns in more specific detail than suggested by metapsychological language. The characteristic means of distorting information processing were described and the ways and degrees of change in these patterns were asserted. Learning was emphasized as an addition to working through. The alteration in information processing allowed revision of meaning structure, as conceptualized in terms of predominant patterns of self and object schematization.

REFERENCES

Berne, E. (1961). *Transactional Analysis in Psychotherapy.* New York: Grove Press.

Easser, B. R., and Lesser, S. R. (1965). Hysterical personality: a re-evaluation. *Psychoanalytic Quarterly* 34:390–405.

Fairbairn, W. R. (1954). Observations on the nature of hysterical states. *British Journal of Medical Psychology* 27:105–125.

Gardner, R. W., Holzman, P. S., Klein, G. S., Linton, H. B., and Spence, D. P. (1959). *Cognitive Control: A Study of Individual Consistencies in Cognitive Behavior.* New York: International Universities Press.

Gedo, J. E., Sabshin, M., Sadow, L., Schlessinger, N., et al. (1964). Studies on hysteria: a methodological evaluation. *Journal of the American Psychoanalytic Association* 12:734–751.

Gedo, J., and Goldberg, A. (1973). *Models of the Mind.* Chicago: University of Chicago Press.

Greenson, R. (1965). The working alliance and the transference neurosis. *Psychoanalytic Quarterly* 34:155–181.

Horowitz, M. J. (1970). *Image Formation and Cognition.* New York: Appleton-Century-Crofts.

_____ (1972). Modes of representation of thought. *Journal of the American Psychoanalytic Association* 20:793–819.

_____ (1974). Microanalysis of working through in psychotherapy. *American Journal of Psychiatry* 131:1208–1212.

_____ (1986). *Stress Response Syndromes.* 2nd ed. Northvale, NJ: Jason Aronson.

_____ (1987). *States of Mind: Analysis of Change in Individual Personality.* 2nd ed. New York: Plenum.

_____ (1988). *Introduction to Psychodynamics: A New Synthesis.* New York: Basic Books.

Horowitz, M. J., and Becker, S. S. (1972). Cognitive response to stress: experimental studies of a compulsion to repeat trauma. In *Psychoanalysis and Contemporary Science*, vol. I, ed. R. Holt and E. Peterfreund, pp. 258–305. New York: Macmillan.

Jacobson, E. (1954). *The Self and Object World*. New York: International Universities Press, 1964.

Kelly, G. (1955). *The Psychology of Personal Constructs*. Vol. 2. New York: Norton.

Kernberg, O. (1966). Structural derivatives of object relationships. *International Journal of Psycho-Analysis* 47:236–253.

_____ (1970). Factors in the psychoanalytic treatment of narcissistic personalities. *Journal of the American Psychoanalytic Association* 18:51–85.

Klein, G. S. (1967). Peremptory ideation: structure and force in motivated ideas. *Psychoanalytic Issues* 5:80–128.

Klein, G. S., et al. (1962). Tolerance for unrealistic experiences: a study of the generality of a cognitive control. *British Journal of Psychology* 53:41–55.

Knapp, P. H. (1974). Segmentation and structure in psychoanalysis. *Journal of the American Psychoanalytic Association* 22:4–36.

Kohut, H. (1968). The psychoanalytic treatment of narcissistic personality disturbances. *Psychoanalytic Study of the Child* 23.

_____ (1971). *The Analysis of the Self*. New York: International Universities Press.

Lazarus, R. S. (1966). *Psychological Stress and the Coping Process*. New York: McGraw-Hill.

Loevinger, J. (1973). *Ego Development*. San Francisco: Jossey-Bass, 1976.

Loewald, H. W. (1960). On the therapeutic action of psychoanalysis. *International Journal of Psycho-Analysis* 41:16–26.

Marmor, J. (1953). Orality in the hysterical personality. *Journal of the American Psychoanalytic Association* 1:656–671.

Miller, G. A., Galanter, E., and Pribram, K. (1960). *Plans and the Structure of Behavior*. New York: Holt.

Myerson, P. (1969). The hysterics's experience in psychoanalysis. *International Journal of Psycho-Analysis* 50:373–384.

Peterfreund, E. (1971). *Information, Systems and Psychoanalysis.* New York: International Universities Press.

Piaget, J. (1937). *The Construction of Reality in the Child.* New York: Basic Books, 1954.

Rapaport, D., and Gill, M. M. (1959). The points of view and assumptions of metapsychology. *International Journal of Psycho-Analysis* 40:153–162.

Sampson, H., and Weiss, J. (1972). Defense analysis and the emergence of warded-off mental contents: an empirical study. *Archives of General Psychiatry* 26:524–532.

Schafer, R. (1968). *Aspects of Internalization.* New York: International Universities Press.

Shapiro, D. (1965). *Neurotic Styles.* New York: Basic Books.

Thompkins, S. (1962). *Affect, Imagery, Consciousness.* New York: Springer.

Wallerstein, R. S. (1986). *Forty-two Lives in Treatment.* New York: Guilford Press.

Wallerstein, R. S., and Sampson, H. (1971). Issues in research in the psychoanalytic process. *International Journal of Psycho-Analysis* 52:11–50.

Weiss, J. (1967). The integration of defences. *International Journal of Psycho-Analysis* 48:520–524.

—— (1971). The emergence of new themes: a contribution to the psychoanalytic theory of therapy. *International Journal of Psycho-Analysis* 52:459–467.

Wisdom, J. O. (1961). A methodological approach to the problem of hysteria. *International Journal of Psycho-Analysis* 42:224–237.

Zetzel, E. (1970). Therapeutic alliance in the analysis of hysteria. In *The Capacity for Emotional Growth,* ed. E. Zetzel, pp. 182–196. New York: International Universities Press.

Index